BOOKS BY REINHOLD NIEBUHR

Man's Nature and His Communities
A Nation So Conceived
            (WITH ALAN HEIMERT)
The Structure of Nations and Empires
Pious and Secular America
The Self and Dramas of History
Christian Realism and Political Problems
The Irony of American History
Faith and History
The Children of Light and the Children
    of Darkness
The Nature and Destiny of Man
Beyond Tragedy
Moral Man and Immoral Society

Reinhold Niebuhr on Politics
EDITED BY HARRY R. DAVIS
AND ROBERT C. GOOD

MAN'S NATURE
AND HIS COMMUNITIES

REINHOLD NIEBUHR

Man's Nature
and His Communities

ESSAYS ON THE DYNAMICS AND
ENIGMAS OF MAN'S PERSONAL
AND SOCIAL EXISTENCE

Charles Scribner's Sons, NEW YORK

TO URSULA

for many reasons

a few of which have been mentioned

in the autobiographical introduction

CONTENTS

CONTENTS

MAN'S NATURE
AND HIS COMMUNITIES

INTRODUCTION:

CHANGING PERSPECTIVES

THIS volume of essays on various aspects of man's individual and social existence is intended to serve two purposes: namely, to summarize, and to revise previously held opinions. They deal with social and political philosophy because that has been the author's chief vocation as a teacher of social ethics in the context of a Protestant theological education, at Union Theological Seminary in New York.

The systematic essays are intended to "revise" previously held opinions only in the sense that they seek to give a systematic account of the revisions which have taken place in the author's mind in a whole lifetime of study and of writing books too frequently. These revisions are of two kinds. On the one hand, they gradually change from a purely Protestant viewpoint to an increasing sympathy for the two other great traditions of Western culture, Jewish and Catholic. They also embody increasingly the insights of the secular disciplines and reflect the author's increasing enthusiasm for the virtues of an open society which allows freedom to all religious traditions, and also the freedom to analyze and criticize all these traditions through the disciplines of an empirical and historical culture.

On the other hand they give an historical (not, I hope, too autobiographical) account of the tortuous path of the author's mind in adjusting the original Protestant heritage of individualism and perfectionism through a world depression and two world wars to the present realities of a highly technical and collective culture, facing the perils of a nuclear age.

The two aspects of revision in my mind were obviously related. I was never a polemical Protestant Christian, trying to score off the Jewish and Catholic faith. But I was increasingly impressed by the fact that both the Jewish and the Catholic faith revealed an awareness of the social substance of man's existence and supplied, in different ways, the norms of justice, which are increasingly required in a collectivist age and which some forms of extravagant Protestantism lack. The latter seem to have two forms of moral norms which stand in contradiction to each other. An ethic of sacrificial love, relevant only to the summit experiences of life, which tends to persuade Christians that they are saints, contrasts with an individualistic-economic ethic of self-reliance which teaches us how to be prosperous.

This latter ethical system became tremendously influential in the early nineteenth-century industrialism, when a moribund Calvinism, placing a prize on the economic virtues, became partner with a social Darwinism. This partnership increased the moral complacency of middle-class America, particularly when the victims of industrial injustice, mostly Catholic and Jewish immigrants, tried vainly to appeal to the conscience of the bourgeoisie.

My appreciation of the Jewish capacity for civic virtue and social justice was not a belated, but an early, insight. It was prompted partly by my experience with Jewish idealists in the political movements, left of center, in which I was engaged. It was prompted partly by the "social gospel" movement, which tried to free the Protestant conscience from undue moral complacency. It did this by the simple expedient of rediscovering the ethic of social justice in the Hebrew prophets.

My first and only pastorate was in Detroit when the new, mass-production auto industry, under the guidance of Henry Ford I, promised to solve all social problems, but aggravated most of them. Later, the world depression and our "New Deal" persuaded a reluctant nation to bring our political system into accord with the moral and social imperatives of modern industry. My mentor and guide was a social-gospel Episcopal Bishop, the late Charles Williams, who was a lonely, dissenting, religious voice in the religious complacency of the city.

In good social-gospel tradition, he refused to join a "Christian Layman's League," which had a program of enforcing stricter Sunday-closing laws. "In the weightier matters of social justice," said the Bishop, "there are only two Christians in Detroit, and they are both Jews." I was puzzled about the sources of the Jewish capacity for social justice. My social-gospel training naturally prompted me to ascribe it to the prophetic inheritance in Judaism. The more observant Jews derived it from the sense of the law, but the irrelevance of much of both Jewish and Christian legalism made this clue dubious.

A marvelous Jewish vice-chairman of the first interracial commission in Detroit, of which I was chairman and which tried to alleviate the post-war racial tensions in the city, had a simple answer to the question concerning this Jewish capacity for social justice. He said that the Jews were inclined by their minority status to be critical of any establishment and sympathetic to any deprived minority. His answer did not exhaust the mystery of the Jewish socio-moral virtues; but I will leave the problem, partly because

Fred Butzel's capacity for magnanimity and social shrewdness was so impressive that it began my long love affair with the Jewish people.

My increasing admiration for the Catholic faith had the same socially pragmatic prompting. Catholics, unlike many Protestants, never had any doubt about the social substance of human existence. The Roman Catholic faith derived much of its "natural law" tradition from classical sources. Since the natural law was intended to give moral norms for a community, it naturally emphasized justice as the relevant norm, though there were differences between the radical Stoic conceptions of equal justice and the later adjustments drawn from Aristotle, through which natural-law theories justified feudal inequalities.

I have not revised my criticism that natural-law moral theories, drawn from a metaphysical base, are too inflexible. They cannot, for instance, adjust the prohibition of contraception to the moral necessities of a population explosion in a rapidly spreading technical culture. But I have a new appreciation of the fact that a great religious tradition, emancipated from the organic collectivism of the Middle Ages, has been able creatively to help modern technical cultures of the West to solve the moral problems of industrial collectivism. As a result, the Roman

Catholic Church never lost the loyalty of its industrial workers. These workers in Protestant cultures often became infected with the virus of the Marxist rebellion. I have made much in the past of the fact that modern social and cultural forces were needed to free the church from the civilization it had itself conceived. I would not revise these judgments, but I do have a new appreciation of the moral and spiritual values which the ancient and universal church contributes to the spiritual and political climate of the open societies. It was inclined to disapprove of democracy in principle. But the Second Vatican Council may be in the process of writing a new chapter on the issue of freedom of conscience.

It must be added that, in these days in which the entire nation is attempting, in the civil-rights struggle, to come to terms with the "American Dilemma" (that is, the contradiction between our professed religious, moral, and political ideals and the sorry deprivation of rights for our Negro minority) the Catholic Church has another claim to our admiration. It has been more consistently universalist, and has championed the "human rights" of all our citizens. An essay in this volume analyzes this problem in more detail. I hope that my Protestant, Jewish, and Catholic friends will not be too shocked by the wholly pragmatic sources of my appreciations.

They come from a teacher of social ethics, and they may claim a classical justification, embodied in Jesus' observation, "by their fruits shall ye know them."

My second account of a gradual revision of my originally held opinions must deal, of course, with my rather violent, and sometimes extravagant, reaction to what I defined as the "utopianism," i.e., the illusory idealist and individualist character, of a Protestant and bourgeois culture before the world depression and two world wars. I must confess to some radical contradictions in my attitudes before I reached the comparatively stable and, I think, valid "realist" and social emphasis that I seek to justify in these essays. For instance, my social-gospel background made my first reaction to the Versailles peace a reaction of pacifist perfectionism. And my reaction to bourgeois individualism prompted me to the error of using Marxist ideas to emphasize our new collective realities. I can only say in self-defense that, despite these absurd inconsistencies, I did succeed in escaping all the hallucinations of the left, who hailed the Russian Revolution as an emancipation for all mankind without noting that its annulment of freedom made the Stalinist despotism almost inevitable.

If I mention the fact that I dimly foresaw the evil roots of this new monopoly of power, it must be because I became so conscious of my many mistakes in my revolt against secular and Christian individualism. I made so many mistakes that I now pathetically seek to claim credit for avoiding the cardinal mistake of many on the left. I must hasten to add that my achievement was by no means unique. My old socialist comrades were in the toils of pacifist illusions, but democratic socialism was always rigorously anti-totalitarian. Thus the rightist doctrine that socialism was but a half-way house to Communism was always purely libelous.

My first venture in political philosophy, published in 1932, was entitled *Moral Man and Immoral Society*. Its thesis was the obvious one, that collective self-regard of class, race, and nation is more stubborn and persistent than the egoism of individuals. This point seemed important, since secular and religious idealists hoped to change the social situation by beguiling the egoism of individuals, either by adequate education or by pious benevolence. A young friend of mine recently observed that, in the light of all the facts and my more consistent "realism" in regard to both individual and collective behavior, a better title might have been *The Not So Moral Man in His Less Moral Communities*.

Meanwhile the world depression and the rise of the Nazi terror swept away the last remnants of liberal utopianism. Having been invited to give the

Gifford Lectures in Edinburgh on the very eve of the Second World War, I inevitably sought to give a theological frame to the now pervasive realism. The lectures, subsequently published under the title *The Nature and Destiny of Man,* sought to describe the biblical-Hebraic description of the human situation, particularly in the symbols of "the image of God in man" and man as "sinner." In the large essay, bearing the title of this present volume, I make the effort to portray the double effects, good and evil, individual and social, of the unique freedom with which human beings are endowed. I hope that my account in this volume has profited in some degree from the debates and criticism prompted by my Gifford Lectures.

I made a rather unpardonable pedagogical error in *The Nature and Destiny of Man,* which I hope I have corrected in the present volume. My theological preoccupation prompted me to define the persistence and universality of man's self-regard as "original sin." This was historically and symbolically correct. But my pedagogical error consisted in seeking to challenge modern optimism with the theological doctrine which was anathema to modern culture. I was in fact proud and heedless because I had taken pains to deny the historicity of the primitive myth of the fall of Adam in the garden, which Paul had associated with the doctrine of original sin, and I also disavowed Augustine's horrendous conception that sin was transmitted from generation to generation through lust in the act of procreation.

But these labors of modern interpretation of traditional religious symbol proved vain. The reaction to my "realism" taught me much about the use of traditional symbols. The remnants of social optimism pictured me as a regressive religious authoritarian, caught in the toils of an ancient legend. But it was even more important that the "realists," including many, if not most, political philosophers who were in substantial agreement with positions taken in my Gifford Lectures, were careful to state that their agreement did not extend to my "theological presuppositions." This present volume, dealing with the same human nature, will understandably use more sober symbols of describing well-known facts. I still think the "London Times Literary Supplement" was substantially correct when it wrote some years ago: "The doctrine of original sin is the only empirically verifiable doctrine of the Christian faith."

A second problem for me, arising from my Edinburgh lectures, had to do with my strong conviction that a realist conception of human nature should be made the servant of an ethic of progressive justice and should not be made into a bastion of conservatism, particularly a conservatism which defends un-just privileges.

I might define this conviction as the guiding prin-ciple throughout my mature life of the relation of religious responsibility to political affairs. The pres-ent volume is an additional testimony to the convic-tion that the future of democracy does not depend upon mild illusions about human virtues and moral capacities. Of course, a Christian with a tradition rooted in the Reformation must make no bones about the fact that the "realism" of the early Reformation led to the arrest of free governments by its political absolutism, its undue reverence for any established political authority (however unjust), and by both Calvin's and Luther's prohibition of resistance even to unjust governments. Let us confess that Cath-olic, Jewish, and secular critics were right in regard-ing these doctrines of the early Reformation as po-litically disastrous.

Millions of Protestants, who are now the dedicated exponents of democracy in the open societies of west-ern European culture, may be entitled to overcome their embarrassment about the political absolutism of the early Reformation by pointing to seventeenth-century Calvinism. It extricated the churches of the Reformation from undue reverence for national po-litical authority. It not only allowed but enjoined resistance to tyranny as a religious obligation. The sects, Calvinist or non-Calvinist, of the Cromwellian revolution elaborated a doctrine of resistance to tyranny which took account of the realities of power, as John Locke's rather individualistic social-contract theory did not.

John Milton, the heretical Calvinist of the Cromwellian revolution, neatly turned the Reformation doctrine of "evangelical liberty," which was politically harmless though religiously meaningful, into a full-fledged doctrine of civil liberty, the pinnacle of the theory of freedom in an open society. Using the same text with which Luther severed religious liberty from political responsibility, Milton said, "My conscience I have from God, and I cannot give it to Caesar." Thus Milton established the true relation of Protestant individualism to an open society. He affirmed in effect that the transcendent freedom of the individual conscience must be recognized by the freedom which the community gives to the individual for the sake of affirming a higher loyalty than the loyalty defined by the "Caesars" of the community. Many complexities of the two dimensions of human existence, individual and social, are not solved by this assertion of freedom as a natural right. But, after Milton, liberty was recognized as one of the regulative principles of justice, together with the older principle of equality.

Perhaps it is unnecessary to rehearse these historic facts. But the diversity of the influences which entered into a politics of justice must serve to remind us that only a great multitude of diverse, and sometimes contradictory, traditions can serve to illumine the meaning and mystery of human existence.

I must close this introduction with an obviously autobiographical conclusion about my increasing devotion to the principles of religious pluralism in an open society which allows the various religious faiths and traditions to contribute their treasures to our common fund. This pluralism must necessarily include the right of non-believers to convict the believers when faith is not fruitful of justice. It also includes the right and duty of the empirical and historical disciplines to subject religious symbols to scrutiny and criticism. Without this latter development, religious traditions may, and frequently do, degenerate from an obscurantist degradation of faith as "basic trust" into faith as belief, belief in propositions which may be historically dubious, though the symbols are the bearers of the meaning of the mystery of human existence.

All this is so obvious to the cultured part of our community, significantly partly religious and partly secular, that my autobiographical promise seems unfulfilled. I hasten to fulfill it.

Since I was always critical of my own tradition

and always appreciative of the Jewish tradition and, more recently, the Catholic tradition, I fain would claim these insights as my own. But the woman I married taught biblical literature to classes containing students of all three major faiths, and she taught courses on "Religion in the Contemporary Culture" in which she drew on all the resources of a liberal arts college as represented by the disciplines of her esteemed colleagues. In other words, the whole cultural climate of her teaching at Barnard College corresponded to the ideal of an open society, such as I have described.

Writing these lines in my old age and being conscious of the spiritual and intellectual debt I owe my wife, not to speak of more precious debts incurred in decades of a happy marriage, I must close this autobiographical introduction with a confession. I do not know how much Ursula is responsible for modifying my various forms of provincialism and homiletical polemics. But I know she is responsible for much of my present viewpoint and that it would be difficult for either of us to mark any opinion expressed in these pages as the unique outlook of one or the other. This volume is the fruit of a lifetime of study in the field of social ethics and political philosophy, dealing with problems we have discussed together and in which we have had parallel interests. I know my wife is the more diligent student of biblical literature and of the relation of psychology to literature and social dynamics. I cannot, therefore, promise that this summary of my lifework is strictly my own. I will not elaborate an already too intimate, autobiographical detail of a happy marriage except to say that this volume is published under my name, and the joint authorship is not acknowledged except in this confession. I will leave the reader to judge whether male arrogance or complete mutuality is the cause of this solution.

MAN'S NATURE

AND HIS COMMUNITIES

A CRITICAL SURVEY OF IDEALIST AND REALIST POLITICAL THEORIES

MAN is both a social and a rational creature. He shares his social character with some animals who live in herds and with insects who exist in hives. The fact that all animals are not social reveals man's greater dependence on the community. His rational character is, of course, uniquely human. He is able to break the tight social harmonies of nature, to project ends beyond the limits of natural impulse. He is able to transmute the natural impulse for survival, which he shares with all creatures, into different forms of self-realization, embodying the pride, vanity, and will-to-power of the human ego. This freedom over natural impulse makes man, who is undoubtedly a creature of nature, into a creator of, and agent in, history. Human communities therefore are subject to endless variations and expansions, while animal communities are nonhistorical in the ageless identity of the form and substance of their social existence.

The effect of human freedom upon man's social impulse and existence is the source of contradictory theories of human behavior. Realists emphasize the disruptive effect of human freedom on the community. Bergson expresses the thesis of Romantic Realism in the words, "When man first begins to think, he thinks of himself first." The idealists, on the other hand, regard man's rational freedom primarily in terms of its creative capacity to extend the limits of man's social sense and to bring order out of the confusion of his impulses and out of the chaos of his conflicting social ambitions, and to give preference to his "moral" or social sense over his self-regard. Kant's conception of the intelligible self as the source of law for the "sensible self" is probably the most succinct statement of the inherent virtue of reason.

The most consistent theories, whether realist or idealist, of political behavior fail to observe the intricate relation between the creative and the disruptive tendencies of human freedom. The realists are inclined to obscure the residual moral and social sense even in the most self-regarding men and nations.

The idealists of both religious and secular persuasion are inclined to obscure the residual individual and collective self-regard either in the "saved" or in the rational individuals and groups. Rational idealism puts its trust in the indeterminate growth of the rational capacity in human history. Religious idealism puts its trust in the redeeming power of the religious experience in giving preference to the social impulse over the self-regarding impulse and to the influence of the special "community of grace" in lifting the social behavior of men to wider breadth and purer expression.

It may be indicative of the double effect of human freedom on the social substance of human existence that the family, which is so obviously the most primordial of human communities and thus becomes the "natural" base for all historical elaborations of the social impulse, is itself an historical product. Aristotle, who, as did most of the Greek philosophers, believed that both natural and historical forms were unchangeable, was thus prompted to an erroneous analogy between animal and human communities, deriving both from the sexual partnership between male and female. Aristotle wrote, ". . . there must be a union of those who can not exist without each other; namely, of male and female, that the race may continue, (and this is a union which is formed, not of deliberate purpose, but because in common with

other animals and with plants, mankind have a natural desire to leave behind an image of themselves)." *

Aristotle's analogy between animal and human
communities is in error. Men indeed share the sexual
impulse and the desire of procreation with the animals, but share the social impulse with only some animals and insects. The sexual partnership between
male and female in animal nature, to which Aristotle refers, is not created until historical development
makes the vagrant male, whose share in procreation
is too minimal to have social effects, a genuine partner of the mother, who is the more obvious parent
of the offspring. Furthermore, the longer dependence
of the children upon their parents, the result of
the slower maturing of learned rather than instinc-
tive responses, really created the family community
among mankind. It is therefore a uniquely human
product and is not shared with the animals. Perhaps
animal herds are more analogous to the kinship communities which grew out of the most primordial of
human communities than to the family. But every
extension of community in history embodies some
contrivance of priest, soldier, and statecraft, designed

* *Politics,* Book I, chap. ii, sec. 2 (from *Basic Works of Aristotle,* ed. Richard McKeon, New York: Random House,
1941).

to extend, circumvent, or suppress a more "natural" form of cohesion.

In his further analysis of the structure of the family community, Aristotle rightly emphasizes that the authority of the father, rather than a pure sense of kinship within the family, is a force of order; but Aristotle commits the familiar error of regarding the dominion of the father as primordial, when probably matriarchy preceded male dominion in actual history for the obvious reason that the mother's relation to the offspring was more patent and potent in primitive communities than that of the father. He quotes Homer to the effect that "each one gives law to his children and to his wives," and thus establishes the father's authority as normative. Paternal authority, even more than the family itself, is not only an historical development but a comparatively late one. Even before the age of the philosophers, the Greek dramatists portrayed themes in which the echoes of a previous struggle between the original matriarchal and the emerging patriarchal forms of family authority were reflected. This difficulty in positing primordial or other norms for the family, or any other human community, may be regarded as indicative of the bewildering confusion in the effects of human freedom on natural forces of cohesion or authority. Luther was quite oblivious of these complex facts when he simply posited paternal authority as one of the unfailing norms of an "order of creation." The same or similar errors were committed by all Stoic and other efforts to equate the "nature" of historical forms with their original and unspoiled manifestation. If it was really original, it was wanting in a developed freedom. If it was obviously historical, it revealed both corruptions and advances upon the original form.

While Aristotle's emphasis on the authority of the father and his derivation of that authority from the paternal impulse to dominion is roughly in the "realist" tradition, his description of the *polis,* the symbol in Greek thought of the civil community, is by contrast an idealistic one because it ascribes the order of the *polis* to a rationally conceived constitution. He writes: "A social instinct is implanted in all men by nature, and yet he who first founded the state was the greatest of all benefactors." *

The idea that the social order of the *polis* represented the triumph of a rational form over the confusion of impulses is of course a theory which Aristotle shares with Plato, whose *Republic* explicitly puts the self and the *polis* into complete analogy, the one governed by reason, the *logisticon,* and the other by the philosopher-king and the guardians. In

* *Ibid.,* sec. 15.

35

both cases, reason is the ordering force over the confusion of natural impulses.

The rational conception of order in Aristotle and Plato did not deal with the impulse of power as the source of both faction and civil order in actual Greek history. It was strong enough to prompt the great Athenian historian Thucydides to observe: "Of the gods we believe, and of men we know, that by a necessary law of their nature they rule wherever they can." *

The confidence in the virtue and power of reason as the source of the social and moral order in the thought of the Greek philosophers did not prompt them to a consistent "idealistic" political theory. Their social theory propounded a strong, even absolutist, government by an élite which would hold the conflicting passions and emotions of the common people in check. Only when the much later Renaissance and Enlightenment hoped for the gradual development and diffusion of the rational faculty as the cause of the concomitant growth of ever larger and more harmonious communities did confidence in reason become the source of idealistic political theories.

Both Plato and Aristotle took the aristocratic social structure and the contingent parochial character

---

* *History of the Peloponnesian War,* Book 5, chap. 105.

of the Greek city-state for granted. They thereby revealed that reason never operates in a vacuum, and that the presuppositions with which it begins—individual or social—make it the servant, rather than the master, of the vital impulses of human life. This ideological taint in the operation of the rational faculty, which refutes all consistent idealistic political theories that derive their optimism from confidence in a developing reason, was not analyzed until the nineteenth century, when both Freud and Marx elaborated their theories of rationalization and ideology.

Freud saw the rational self, the ego, as an uneasy broker between the clamant impulses of the id, roughly analogous to the various natural or animal impulses of Plato's *epithymeticon,* and the superego, or the moral authority of the community—though *what* community remains in doubt. In any case, the Freudian theory of rationalization did not deal with the ambitions and desires of the conscious ego. It was therefore only indirectly relevant to political theory. Marx saw the ideological taint—that is, the ambiguity of the rational faculty—purely as a class phenomenon, and interpreted the class interests, which were consciously or unconsciously served by the rationalization of interests, as purely economic, rather than as being the more obvious and dominant political phenomenon of the will-to-power. He therefore erroneously ascribed the ideological taint only to the property owners, the bourgeoisie, and promised redemption through the abolition of the institution of property. To compound his errors, Marx posited a redemption of the whole community through a proletarian class, the rational purity of which was guaranteed by its lack of property interests.

Naturally, this polemical version of political realism obscured all the complex interactions between the rational and the vital impulses, and the double consequence of social creation and social confusion in both impulses. It therefore created an apocalyptic vision of social redemption, rather than an empirical analysis of complex and intricate relations of human and social impulses.

Marxist utopianism, despite its many novel factors as a religio-political form of Messianism, is really an old form of religious self-righteousness, and combines the two forms of interpretation with which we are concerned—realism and idealism. Thus, Marxism is realistic about the human nature and behavior of the "sinners," the competitors, the bourgeoisie, but is idealistic about the "redeemed" group, in this case not the church or the chosen nation, but the Messianic class.

The original moral and spiritual framework for the interpretation of human nature and the organization of the human community was given by the Christian faith in the Western culture. We must therefore turn to an analysis of Christian moral and political theory and life with its bewildering confusion of realism and idealism, and of valid and invalid combinations of the two theories.

In principle, the Christian faith holds that human nature contains both self-regarding and social impulses and that the former is stronger than the latter. This assumption is the basis of Christian realism. It must not be assumed that the virtue inherent in this realistic analysis of the human condition guarantees the validity of any Christian solution for two vexing problems: the establishment of a tolerable harmony between self-regarding individuals within the civil community, and the relations of integral political communities with each other. The second problem is naturally more difficult than the first because of the strength of collective self-regard in comparison with the self-regard of individuals.

The Christian faith came into existence against the background of the older Hebrew faith. Hebrew faith was based upon the covenant of God with his people Israel. The prophets from the eighth century B.C. on, in different ways and in different degrees, projected this faith into the ideal of a Messianic age. This ideal expressed all the hopes of human fulfillment where man would live with man in a univer-

sal and peaceful community, and all the frustra-
tions and contradictions of history would be
eliminated.

These Messianic hopes may be described as "idealistic," for they express the desires and impulses of
man acting freely, and not totally bound either by
his historical and particular situation or by his own
self-regard.

Hebraic and later Christian Messianism runs as a
major theme throughout Western history, remind-
ing us that "man's reach is" always "beyond his
grasp." But if the original religious hope of a trans-
formed nature, as the basis for a fulfilled historical
community, be lost, the result then is utopianism.
Thus the religious traditions of the West, both Jewish and Christian, are potential generators of an idealistic utopian vision, creative in projecting ultimate
and ideal goals for human communities, but confusing whenever they obscure the perennial force of the
factors in human nature which prevent the fulfill-
ment of these ideal goals.

There was another emphasis, however, in the
faith of the early Christian church. Paul and other
writers of the New Testament declare that Jesus,
who died upon the cross, was the Messiah. The tri-
umphant Messiah and the suffering servant, these
were the two great ideal figures of Jewish hope, and

Christian faith saw them combined and realized in the person of Jesus. According to the New Testament, therefore, the Messianic Age did not fulfill the ideal potentialities of human nature and history but offered instead a "reconciliation" between God and man. Man, as individual and also in relationship with his fellows and his community, always is contradicting and defying the law of love. This law, the command both of Torah and Gospel, also is the ultimate law of human existence. Thus the story of the life of Jesus with the death on the cross became, for Christianity, the initial statement of a "realistic" interpretation of human history.

This "realism" is also expressed in the Pauline description of the tension between the impulses of self-regard and love in the soul of each individual. Thus, "I delight in the law of God, in my inmost self, but I see in my members another law at war with the law of my mind . . ." (ROMANS 7:22-23). It is further emphasized by his confession that the strength of self-regard is greater than the strength of conscience committed to the "law of God," obviously the law of love or the social impulse: "For I do not do the good I want, but the evil that I do not want is what I do" (ROMANS 7:19).

The Pauline and Christian solution for this inner moral problem stated so realistically was, however, a source of confusion in the political thought of the West. The divine grace mediated by Christ, who expressed the ultimate resources available to repentant man who confesses his desperate situation, contained both new power and pardon. The power of a new life was the power of complete sacrificial love, as explicated by the drama of Christ's death: "I have been crucified with Christ; it is no longer I who live, but Christ who lives in me" (GALATIANS 2:20). This new life in Christ represents the perfection of complete and heedless self-giving which obscures the contrary impulse of self-regard. It is a moral ideal scarcely possible for the individual and certainly not relevant to the morality of self-regarding nations.

Paul manifested both idealistic and realistic moods, derived from his theory of grace, as being the power of a new and selfless life—"If any one is in Christ, he is a new creation" (II CORINTHIANS 5:17)—and also as the mercy shown by God to all men who, in even a redeemed state, will continue to defy the law of God.

In his idealistic moods, Paul made perfect love (*Agape,* the love of God for man) into the new and higher standard of the "new Israel," the redeemed community, the church, which was the "body of Christ" (I COR. 12-13). In his realistic moods, he conceded that the new community would have to deal with a morally ambiguous human nature, and civil society must have the higher "authority" from God "to execute his wrath on the wrongdoer," to "restrain the evil," this higher authority being "instituted by God" (ROM. 13:1,4). This realist sanctification of civil authority was to be fatefully used, particularly by the Reformation, to induce an uncritical reverence for established authority, however unjust.

Paul's idealism and realism were extravagantly expressed by his chief disciples, Augustine and Luther, in a dualism in which the standard of love among the redeemed took no account of the persistence of self-love in the lives of the "redeemed" or of the residual virtue and sense of social responsibility in the lives of the unredeemed individuals. Augustine's classic *De Civitate Dei* related the Pauline concept of *Agape,* or perfect love, to a mythical *Civitas Dei,* and thereby transmuted it into a neo-Platonic *Amor Dei.* He was uncertain whether or not this mythical kingdom of perfect virtue was identical with the historic church, although his denials of the identity were more numerous than his hints of identity.

On the other hand, the Augustinian *Civitas Terrena* was the first and most rigorous expression of Christian realism. This had, however, the defect of all consistent realistic accounts of human behavior.

Relations in this "city" were governed purely by self-love, by an uneasy armistice between contending interests and by the provisional peace caused by the momentary victory of a dominant political force. Unlike Paul before him, and Luther after him, Augustine failed to accord divine sanction to established civil authority.

Augustine's thesis demanded that he challenge Cicero's Stoic and idealistic picture of the *Pax Romana* as a compact of justice. Cicero had obscured the elements of power in the Roman dominion. Augustine countered by emphasizing those elements to the exclusion of the genuine achievements of justice in Roman law. It was neither the first nor the last time that realistic and idealistic versions of a complex reality missed the intricacies in the political order.

But the Augustinian logic required that he should challenge Roman authority insofar as it was based on power. This he did on the basis of Stoic equalitarianism, relegated by the Stoics to a mythical Golden Age for the obvious reason that the historic facts and necessities contradicted it. Unlike the Stoics, who regarded the economic and political instruments of community after the Golden Age as necessities of justice, Augustine regarded them as instruments of sin.

44

Luther, obviously indebted to Augustine's conception in his *Civitas Dei,* elaborated a different idea in his two realms, but he was equally extravagant in both his realism and idealism.

Luther's "heavenly realm" was not the realm of those who love God rather than self. It was a realm of perfect sacrificial and forgiving love among individual Christians who felt themselves forgiven. The "earthly realm," however, was clearly Augustine's *Civitas Terrena,* the "realm of Caesar"—in short, the political and collective realm which Luther conceived as an area of purely coercive restraint in "sinful" or self-regarding men; of "chains, courts, the law and the sword." His realism, expressed in this earthly realm, was even more extravagant than Augustine's because he provided divine sanction for the political authority which restrained recalcitrant individuals.

The realm of Caesar was inhabited by consistently self-regarding men, as in the Augustinian *Civitas Terrena.* These men were as devoid of a sense of justice as the heavenly kingdom was devoid of a need for justice in a community of pure self-giving.

By appealing to Jesus' words, "Render to Caesar the things that are Caesar's, and to God the things that are God's," Luther insists on the radical contrast between the two realms, although they represent only two dimensions of human existence. Civic order is attained in the political realm by pure repression, the God-ordained *Obrigkeit,* using "chains, laws, courts, and the sword."

Unlike Augustine, Luther conceives of the civil authority not merely as a dominant power, but as a sanctified authority. He appeals to the authority of Scripture (i.e., Paul's observation in ROMANS 13 about the higher authority being instituted by God) and also draws its sanctity from the fact that it is derived from the authority of the father, which Luther erroneously considers a part of the "order of creation." The analogy does violence to the contrast between the benignity of paternal authority and the repressive and forceful instruments of power in the hands of civil authority. The analogy was nevertheless so popular in Reformation thought that John Locke devoted one section of his *Two Treatises of Government* to a refutation of its legitimacy.

Whatever may be said about the resources of the Christian faith in transmuting and guiding the lives of individuals, an analysis of Augustine's and Luther's dualism and consequent "realism" affecting political communities must yield the negative conclusion that the realism was too consistent to give a true picture of either human nature or the human community, even before the advent of free governments, and was certainly irrelevant to modern democratic governments.

In comparison, the "idealist" version of human nature and of man's community in medieval Catholicism, against which Luther reacted, seems to be closer to the truth. Its obvious advantages were numerous. It relegated the politically irrelevant gospel perfectionism to the category of "counsels of perfection," normative only for monastics and ascetics, or in any case for those who had no responsibility for collective interests and values, whether of family or civil community. This emphasis on celibacy and on irresponsible virtue has grave faults as a guide to personal conduct. Partially prompted by the traditional negative attitude toward man's sexual life, it makes a dubious distinction between two degrees of Christian perfection, encourages self-righteousness of first-degree Christians, and assumes that moral perfection can be achieved by rigorous discipline and not by the grace of a community which redeems mankind of self-concern.

But politically, Catholic asceticism has the virtue of recognizing a fact which other perfectionists do not recognize, namely, that collective responsibility and collective self-concern begin with the family's, not with the civil community's, alter-egoism. Therefore, a highly individualistic ethic, drawn from the individual relations in the most primordial of communities, the family, is only indirectly relevant to a social ethic having the task of establishing norms of justice for competing, collective interests in the civil community. An ancillary political advantage is that the monastic tradition removes from civil responsibility those sensitive spirits who are in perpetual agony about the moral ambiguities of all political norms and practices.

Although Catholic thought explicitly placed individual perfection beyond the realm of political and collective morality and drew its norms from the concept of the "natural law," nevertheless it must be placed in the category of "political idealism." Three emphases of medieval thought constitute its nature as nonrealistic political theory:

(a) It is sufficiently Platonic, in common with such diverse thinkers as Spinoza, Kant, and Freud, to regard the "passions" of man's animal nature, rather than the will-to-power of the ego, as the forces of human nature which defy the law.

(b) It conceives the natural law as a system of norms without considering that historical norms are influenced by the contingent power factors in an historical situation.

(c) It assumes that the authority of the church, which enforces the norms of the natural law, is the authority of collective conscience rather than of power; and it believes that the church is identical with the universal human community, when in fact it was the senior partner of a tremendous parochial power structure, the Holy Roman Empire.

Thomas Aquinas defined natural law as "the participation of rational creatures in the eternal law," which is to say, the very order of the world in its natural and historical processes. Medieval thought had, in fact, inherited the concept of natural law from classical philosophy, Stoic and Aristotelian, and shared the classical conviction that both nature and history were governed by inflexible forms, or "universals," through which the natural and historical processes moved in eternal cycles. This classical concept, defined in the Middle Ages as "realism," was at such obvious variance with the facts of both nature and history that it was challenged by "nominalism" before the end of the Middle Ages, and by the natural sciences from the rise of modern astronomy to Darwinian biology.

The fate of Aristotelian deductive science need not concern us in the study of political philosophy, except as an empirical culture is bound to be increasingly nominalistic and therefore is not inclined to accept moral or political norms alleged to be either universal or inflexible. In terms of political philosophy, modern thinkers of every school are bound to be critical of the lack of realism in a system of thought so obviously historically conditioned.

Medieval concepts of natural law especially showed their historical character. The shift from Stoic to Aristotelian concepts appropriately accompanied the development of feudal society with its hierarchy of power, authority and privilege analogous to that of Athenian aristocratic society. The later Middle Ages echoed the dictum of Aristotle, "justice requires that man treat unequal things unequally."

In short, the evidence pointed to the fact that an eternal law could be nothing but a class ideology or rationalization of interest. The fact was obvious long before Marx pointed out that social norms were founded in class interests, even though their pinnacles reached as high as heaven. The rising middle classes and craftsmen, who felt themselves defrauded by the medieval system of social norms, challenged not only the thought but the feudal social system in the bourgeois revolution and its organization of free governments. They also conceived a new system of "natural rights" or "inalienable rights," proclaimed to be self-evident as confidently as the old system of natural law. It proved to be as influenced by bourgeois interests as the old system was by feudal interests.

The ideological taint of self-interest in the most rationally conceived social standards, which James Madison attributed to the "intimate relation of self-love and reason" is, of course, a universal phenomenon which, provisionally at least, validates political realism in its debate with most idealistic theories and certainly with all consistently idealistic theories.

In terms of medieval theory, the church was a "spiritual kingdom." Gregory VII had, in fact, used Augustine's conception of the *Civitas Dei* as the foundation for the grand conception of the medieval papacy and church. In this theory, it did not rule by power. It enforced the precepts of the natural law by (purely) moral authority. In fact, it was the senior partner in the elaborate partnership of church and empire that ruled the whole of medieval culture and social organization. Since Charlemagne's imperial dignity was created by the church, Charlemagne was clearly the junior partner. He was the police arm of the church, since the church, as a spiritual kingdom, could not use force.

The theory which sanctified this peculiar partnership, and church supremacy in the partnership, was stated by John of Salisbury in *Policraticus:* "The place of the head in the body of the commonwealth is filled by the prince, who is subject only to God and to those who exercise His office and represent Him on earth, even as in the human body the head is quickened and governed by the soul." * Thomas Aquinas, the most authoritative theologian of the medieval church, was even more explicit in his *De Regimine Principum:* "In order that spiritual things might be distinguished from earthly things, the ministry of this kingdom (Christ's) has been entrusted not to earthly kings, but to priests, and in the highest degree to the chief priest, the successor of St. Peter, the Vicar of Christ, the Roman Pontiff, to whom all kings of Christian peoples are to be subject as to our Lord Jesus Christ Himself. For those to whom pertains the care of intermediate things, should be subject to whom pertains the care of the ultimate end." †

In short, the structure of power in the supreme authority of medieval Christendom was derived from a religious conception of authority, which veiled the coercive element in the structure. It was the possession of the "keys of heaven" by the Pope that could hold people in thrall by the sanction of excommunication, and kings in awe by the sanction of interdiction, which was the threat of removing the divine sanction of royal authority. It was cer-

---

* John of Salisbury, *Policraticus,* Book IV, 3.
† St. Thomas Aquinas, *On the Governance of Rulers,* trans. by G. B. Phelan.

tainly inevitable that the pretension involved in this structure of authority should have prompted violent and cynical reactions and that the junior partners of the papacy—the emperors—anticipated the Reformation in these reactions, including the violent epithets regarding the Pope as "anti-Christ." They did not, of course, go as far as to define the church as "the whore of Babylon," as did later both Luther and John Knox.

The disintegration of medieval culture and social organization through the rising power of the nations and the commercial classes within the nations, as well as the challenge to ecclesiastical authority by the Renaissance and the Reformation, prompted both idealistic and realistic theories of human behavior and the organization of the civil community. Dante presented, in his *De Monarchia,* a late medieval and early Renaissance idealistic effort to restore Christian universalism by purging it of the pretension of papal supremacy. But Dante's hope of establishing a universal community through an omnipotent, imperial authority was clearly a nostalgic and idealistic illusion. Within a century, Machiavelli's *The Prince* projected a realistic reaction against all previous idealism. He championed or took for granted the parochial community of the Italian city-state, and was indifferent both to the rising nations and to the declining church and empire. But the essential realism of his political theory consisted in his dismissing as visionary all systems of value and political organization not based on obvious parochial sovereignty. He wrote: "It appears to me more appropriate to follow the real truth of the matter rather than the imagination of it, for many have pictured republics and principalities, which in fact were never known or seen." * Inevitably, Machiavelli became the whipping boy of all defenders of the medieval political system. He was denounced as a cynic, and did indeed betray cynical touches in his ambivalent advice to the ruler to seek the appearance of generosity more assiduously than its reality, which raised questions about the possible satirical or serious nature of his sentiments. At any rate, the line between cynicism and realism is not too sharply defined when the realist seeks to unmask the pretensions of the idealist in the power struggles of politics.

In seventeenth-century England, the Cromwellian Revolution produced a variety of theories of human nature and political community. Renaissance humanism contributed some elements. The Reformation bequeathed others. We have considered earlier some of the excesses of Reformation thought, its rigorous

---

* Machiavelli, *The Prince,* trans. W. K. Mariott (London: Everyman's Library, J. M. Dent and Sons Ltd., 1908), p. 121.

dualism, its distinction between the private and the political realm, the "spiritual" and the physical dimension of human existence. The theological view, that the spiritual and private world was virtuous and pure and that the physical and political realm was self-seeking and that it was always so, obscured two important points. It obscured the residual self-regard in the personal and interpersonal realm, and also the residual sense of justice in the collective and political realm.

Two men in seventeenth-century England expressed, in very different ways, concepts from both Renaissance and Reformation thought. Thomas Hobbes and John Locke shared certain concepts but used them for contradictory purposes. Thus, both accepted a mythical "state of nature." For Hobbes, it was a state of social anarchy, of "war of all against all." For Locke, it was a state of "inconvenience" because "men were judges in their own cases."

Further, Hobbes propounded, and Locke took over from him, an equally mythical "social contract" as the beginning of civil community. Both myths obscure the slow growth and development of civil society. Yet, both Hobbes and Locke must have known about this development in which human contrivance is introduced by imperceptible steps and degrees in the forms of social coherence furnished by nature. Thus, the myth of the "social contract" was a symbol of modern man's protest against his subordination to historical and natural ties in a traditional society, and an assertion of man's role as creator and agent in history. The myth vividly but erroneously gathers, into one discrete act of reason and will, all the gradual accretions of human freedom in the historical process.

Hobbes, of course, made the social contract the basis of a political absolutism, while Locke used it as the foundation for modern democratic theory. The contrasting political theories were derived from contrasting and equally mistaken views of the role of reason in man's relation to the community. Reason, for Hobbes, is the servant of interest, and therefore socially disruptive. Making an obvious distinction between animal and human communities, Hobbes argues, "these creatures, having not (as man) the use of reason, they do not see, or think they see, any fault in the administration of their common business. Whereas among men, there are many who think themselves wiser and abler to govern the public better than the rest; and these strive to reform and innovate the one this way and the other one that way, and thereby bring it to distraction and civil war." *

These pessimistic words about human reason's

* Hobbes, *Leviathan, or the Matter, Forme and Power of a Commonwealth, Ecclesiastical and Civil,* ed. with introduction by Michael Oakshott (Oxford: Basil Blackwell, 1955), p. 117.

socially disruptive consequences were written during, and no doubt inspired by, the Cromwellian revolution. It is therefore interesting that they imply the creative function of human rationality, although they emphasize its disruptive consequences. Hobbes, in short, was so alarmed by the confusion of "innovating" sectarians in Cromwell's army that his alarm prompted an absolutist solution for the peril of civil war. Only a strong government, armed with preponderant power, could ensure peace. Hobbes wrote: "It is manifest that during the time men live without a common power to keep them in awe, they are in that condition, which is called warre, and such a warre as is of every man against every man." *

Hobbes's absolutist theory had no relevance to English politics, not only because his realism was an inaccurate description of political behavior, but because the constitutional monarchy was deeply rooted in English history. Its monarchial symbol was the focal point of order, and the growing power of parliament, before and after the Cromwellian revolution, showed that democratic freedom was not as incompatible with the order of the nation as Hobbes had assumed in the chaos of the civil war. Hobbes's realism is therefore significant for the modern student only in displaying the relation between an inexact realist conception of human nature and the conse-

* *Ibid.,* p. 82.

quent erroneous conception of authority. Hobbes emphasized the disruptive, rather than the creative, consequence of rational freedom. The civil authority, ostensibly created by the social contract in which the reason of the community sought to mitigate the disruptive consequences of parochial rationality, was as devoid of the majesty and prestige that would elicit the implicit consent of the ruled as their reason was devoid of any enlargement of sympathy or of a sense of justice.

This coordination in the thought of Hobbes between an extravagant realism in the analysis of human nature and an extravagant absolutism in the conception of civil authority is important because it betrays a defect in many, if not all, realistic theories of political affairs. Hobbes's "power," which was to keep the unruly community in order through awe, was never specifically defined as pure force. But since it was bereft of historical, traditional, and moral majesty, the "awe" which the power elicited was fear rather than reverence for the symbol of the community's majesty.

John Locke, of course, drew democratic conclusions from the social-contract theory, and thereby became the fountainhead of the democratic idealism which would eventually inspire or sanction the democratic revolutions of France, England, and America. Locke expressed the individualistic voluntarism of the bourgeois classes in an extravagant degree. The "social contract" conception, which he inherited from Hobbes, was a compact of individuals calculated not only to create civil order but to protect those "natural rights" which Hobbes would abrogate for the sake of communal order. These defects in the theory cannot, of course, obscure the importance of the clear affirmation that "just governments derive their authority from the consent of the governed."

Locke's individualism and voluntarism were explicit in the error of identifying implicit and explicit consent, thus obscuring all historical and traditional forces which create implicit consent for civil communal authority. His rationalism also blinded him to the ideological taints in the reason by which different factions in the community measure the explicit consent to specific measures of government.

Locke expresses his idealistic and voluntaristic conception of the social contract in this way: "When any number of men have, by the consent of every individual, made a community, they have thereby made the community one body, with a power to act as one body, which is only by the will and determination of the majority." * For Locke, reason without any regard for interest or power is effective in estab-

* *Two Treatises of Government,* ed. with introduction by J. W. Gough (Oxford: Basil Blackwell, 1946), "Second Treatise," chap. viii, par. 96.

lishing and ordering the community. Men do not sacrifice their "freedom from absolute arbitrary power" by entering into the social contract, Locke argues, because this natural right is "so necessary to, and closely joined with, a man's preservation, that he cannot part with it but by what forfeits his preservation and life together." *

Locke's rational idealism prompts him to ignore the whole history of the Cromwellian revolution, including the theories of later Calvinism about the right of resistance to tyranny, and to appeal merely to the "right" to correct injustice. He argues: "Whensoever . . . the legislative shall transgress this fundamental rule of society, and either by ambition, fear, folly, or corruption, endeavor to grasp themselves, or put into the hands of any other, an absolute power over the lives, liberties, and estates of the people; by this breach of trust they forfeit the power the people put into their hands for quite contrary ends, and it devolves to the people, who have a right to resume their original liberty, and by the establishment of a new legislative, (such as they shall think fit), provide for their own safety and security, which is the end for which they are in society." †

* *Ibid.*, "Second Treatise," chap. iv, par. 23.
† *Ibid.*, chap. xix, par. 222.

Locke's confidence both in the inviolability of the "natural right" and in the rational possibility of restoring violated rights, together with his assumption that there is some clear mark of distinction between just and unjust government which "the people" as a whole can discern, laid the foundation for all idealistic liberal theories of politics. These theories obscure the factors of collective interest, for there is power in all communities, and there are endless variations of interest in preserving order while attaining justice in free communities.

Locke was regarded as the philosophical vindicator of the "glorious revolution" in which Parliament asserted and extended its authority by placing William and Mary on the English throne and ending both the confusion of the Cromwellian period and the absolutism of the restoration. Yet, his theories failed to echo the factors, forces, traditions, and accommodations of interests and powers which were operative in the history of English parliamentary democracy and constitutional monarchy, and which fortunately saved England from the illusions of a pure, idealistic liberalism. Meanwhile, the empiricism of David Hume and the moderate conservatism of Edmund Burke provided a more adequate analysis both of human nature and of political community.

In America, the revolution fortunately was also

saved from Lockean principles, which were its original inspiration, not only by many historical factors but also by the thought of such moderate realists as James Madison, the author of the American Constitution, Alexander Hamilton, and John Adams. Only in France did purely Lockean principles prevail, and it was there that consequent Lockean illusions also prevailed. For in France the revolutionary movement, trusting the "authority of the sovereign people" and putting faith in "reason," allowed the obvious effect of interest on "reason" to be obscured, as was also the fact that "interest" inevitably produces faction and dissension in the "sovereign People." The consequent confusion with Jacobin fanaticism and the later flight to Bonapartist despotism illustrates the inevitable tendencies of communities to flee the dangers of anarchy by courting the perils of absolutism.

The differences between the thought of Hobbes and Locke illustrate the relation of theories of government to estimates of human nature. Human freedom always produces disruptive as well as creative effects in the human community. This is understood and also reflected by the common-sense of both statesmen and general public rather more accurately than by a too consistent philosophical theory. But it is important to emphasize again that both types of theory about human nature, while they may be equally wide of the truth about human nature, do have these contradictory consequences in political theory. The pessimistic theory encourages political absolutism by flying from political anarchy to an omni-competent and omnipotent political authority. This alternative, not popular today, represents a nostalgic return to traditional political structures. The theory of idealism, on the other hand, encourages the rise of free governments. Its optimistic estimate of human nature was a necessary source of energy which was needed to challenge traditional forms of authority.

But this initial contribution to the rise of democracy by idealistic liberalism must not obscure the danger of Western democracy becoming unduly dependent upon mild illusions about human nature and the political order. For these illusions obscure the refractory character of man's nature and particularly the stubborn force of his collective self-regard.

The increased power of collective self-interest compared with individual self-interest has been an unsolved problem ever since the Christian realists, Augustine and Luther, relegated the ethic of the interpersonal relations of the family to the heavenly or spiritual realm, and solved the problem of collective relations and harmony by a rigorous "realistic" program of political coercion for the sake of communal harmony.

The rise of bourgeois democracy was in effect the emergence in the political realm of the old religious individualism. But an ironic touch was added to this idealism by the emergence of a new democratic "realism." This realism did not, like the old realism, seek to suppress parochial interests for the sake of the larger good. It sought to harness self-interest to the common good of the civic community, as Alexander Hamilton did when he made it profitable for the wealthy classes to support the new American Constitution. Or it promised justice as the inevitable fruit of competitive striving with nothing but the free market to regulate the self-regarding ambitions of men, as in the theories of classical economy. It even appropriated the biological theories of Darwin in Spencer's social Darwinism, and promised that a rigorous competition between individuals would lead to the survival of the fittest. Thus bourgeois culture presented itself to the world, which was destined progressively to encounter the collective conflicts of modern industry, with a high religious ethic of sacrificial love and a realistic ethic of encouraging "private initiative." The confluence of social Darwinism and moribund Calvinism served to quiet consciences uneasy about the growing disparity between rich and poor under the exaggerated disbalances of power created when the power machine transferred the skill and the tool of the craftsman to the industrial corporation.

The combination of errors was in fact so great in the bourgeois age that it must be regarded as one of the wonders of history that Western democracies did not completely succumb to the Marxist rebellion prompted by the glaring injustices of early industrialism. In this combination, the idealists conceived the democratic government as a purely rational procedure. Its authority was derived from the "consent of the governed," understood as explicit consent. Its encounters were interpreted as a purely rational dialogue of men, without an echo of the collective interests which would guide and corrupt the rational process. Thus Jefferson could extol American democracy: "We exist, and are quoted, as standing proofs that a government so modelled as to rest continually on the will of the whole of society, is a practicable government . . . as members therefore, of the universal society of mankind, and standing in high and responsible relation with them, it is our sacred duty . . . not to blast the confidence we have inspired of proof that a government of reason is better than one of force." * The Lockeans considered

* Andrew Libscomb and Ellery Bergh (eds.), *Writings of Thomas Jefferson* (Washington, D.C.: Thomas Jefferson Memorial Assn., 1903), Vol. XV, p. 284.

neither interest nor power, and had a simple contrast between reason and force.

The realists, on the other hand, acknowledged interest, but denied its collective or class character, and were as afraid of political discipline of economic interests as were the idealists. They hoped that a free market would establish justice. Obviously they were blind to the problem of the disparity of power which prevented laborers and employers from engaging in an equitable bargain. Both the idealists and the realists showed the force of class interests which the idealists were inclined to deny. James Madison was the only one of the founding fathers who made a realistic analysis of both power and interest from a political and democratic perspective. He was governed by a basic insight of political realism, namely the "intimate relation" between reason and self-love. Unlike the idealists, he knew the need for strong government. Unlike Thomas Hobbes, he feared the dangers of strong government and thought that the "separation of powers" in government itself would prevent tyranny. Madison shared the fear of "faction" with all the Founding Fathers, but gave us the best pre-Marxist analysis of the basis of collective and class interests in the varying "talents" and consequent economic interests of various classes. He did not propose to suppress faction but to manage it, because he wisely realized that the price of liberty was the free play of interests in collective terms. Despite these remarkable insights he did not anticipate that Western democracies would organize their procedures through the very "factions," or parties, which the Founding Fathers so much abhorred.

The whole historical process by which Western democracies righted the injustices of early industrialism and established a tolerable harmony of collective interests within the framework of modern industrialism, thus vindicating the dignity and viability of free institutions and the very survival of democracy, is an eloquent testimony more to the virtues of a free society than to the virtues of any of the agents in the process. This triumph of free institutions involved the refutation of bourgeois ideologies which might have proved Western democracy to be as captive to middle-class interests as the Marxists contended. It refuted the bourgeois idealists who pretended that men could engage in politics with a pure and disinterested reason; and that political struggles involved individuals but not classes. It refuted the bourgeois realists who pretended that competition in the market would ensure justice and that bargaining in the labor market would defend the worker's interest, despite the disparity of power between worker and employer.

The whole process extended the right of suffrage to universal dimensions not originally intended by the bourgeois classes, and made the equal political power inherent in the franchise an instrument for equalizing privileges in the economic sphere not anticipated by the middle-class idealists and realists. Perhaps the most important triumph was the final one, when it became apparent that political power was not enough to guarantee economic justice. Then, the pressures of free communities forced the reluctant middle-class employers to allow the workers to organize, bargain collectively, and thus to create a tolerable equilibrium of power between organized industry and organized labor.

This vindication of an open society was made possible through an understanding of the factors of both interest and power. It thus refuted pure idealism so thoroughly that the whole of modern political philosophy may be defined as realistic. However, this whole history also refuted the absolutism of the pre-democratic realists because it revealed that political encounters and debates in a free society involved not only contests of interest and power, but the rational engagement and enlargement of a native sympathy, a sense of justice, a residual moral integrity, and a sense of the common good in all classes of society.

The American War of Independence against an imperial power naturally increased the misconceptions among American idealists about the behavior of nations, and raised the problem of bringing the stubborn self-regard of nations, which has always challenged the beliefs of idealistic liberalism, to a climax. The American liberal tradition solved it simply by regarding the institution of monarchy as the root of all aggressive and expansive attitudes of nations. The Declaration of Independence indicted George III of England in terms which implied that he was an absolute monarch. He was, in fact, a constitutional king, the third in a line of Hanoverian kings who owed their position to an explicit act of Parliament. In short, the chasm between monarchy and democracy was not as deep as the Founding Fathers assumed. Certainly the difference in national behavior between traditional and democratic governments was not as marked as the Fathers assumed.

The liberal illusion that democracies were free of the vice of national ambition and self-regard and that America, as the purest of democracies, was not "imperialistic" was refuted in the first half-century of American history, when the young nation expanded over the whole hemisphere and challenged all other sovereignties in it, under the slogan of "manifest destiny." That slogan merely revealed that the veil of democratic ideals was inevitably used to cover the common, even universal impulses, which America shared with all nations, to increase its dominion and its power.

Despite this obvious refutation and subsequent ones too numerous to mention, liberal and idealistic illusions about the morality of America remained in its national ideology from Thomas Jefferson to the last of the Jeffersonians, Woodrow Wilson. He affirmed that "America is the most unselfish of all nations."

The idealistic interpretation of the morality of nations, more particularly the American, was obviously absurd. It did not deal relevantly with a moral and political problem which modern culture has confronted ever since the rise of autonomous nations at the beginning of the modern period. These nations were integral, parochial communities, not subject to the laws and restraints of larger communities. They possessed all the instruments of sovereignty to enforce their claims upon their own citizens, and presumably all the instruments of force to enforce their claims upon their neighbors and their adversaries. The problem is whether these autonomous nations, free of all external restraints, are also free of all internal moral restraints upon their expansive and self-regarding impulses.

Thus the moral problem of collective self-regard, which began with the family's external rather than internal behavior, has reached its climax in our day. The consistent tendencies of nations to seek their own interests is so marked that the realistic interpretation of international relations would seem to be the only valid description of their behavior, and possibly the only true solution to the problem this behavior poses. Nevertheless it is important to raise once again the question whether a realistic interpretation may not err in obscuring the residual capacity for justice and devotion to the larger good, even when it is dealing with a dimension of collective behavior in which the realistic assumptions about human nature are most justified.

It may be possible to analyze this issue succinctly by examining the thought of the most brilliant and authoritative political realist, Hans Morgenthau, whose magnum opus, *Politics among the Nations,* deals inevitably with the morality of nations.* Morgenthau comes to grips with the ultimate question in collective morality, which might be stated in this way: Are nations capable of being loyal to interests and values other than their own "national interest"?

Morgenthau sometimes answers this question in terms which would seem to suggest that nations are

* New York: Alfred A. Knopf, 1958.

loyal to interests, values, and structures of culture higher than their own interests. He writes:

> International politics, like all politics, is a struggle for power. Whatever the ultimate aims of international politics, power is always the immediate aim. Statesmen and peoples may ultimately seek freedom, security, prosperity or power itself. They may define their goals in terms of a religious, philosophical, economic or social ideal. They may hope that this ideal will materialize through its own inner force, through divine intervention or through the natural development of human affairs. They may also try to further its realization through non-political means, such as technical cooperation with other nations or international organizations. But, whenever they strive to realize their goals by means of international politics, they do so by striving for power. The crusaders wanted to free the holy places from domination by the infidels; Woodrow Wilson wanted to make the world safe for democracy; the National Socialists wanted to open Eastern Europe to German colonization, to dominate Europe, and to conquer the world. Since they all chose power to achieve these ends, they were actors on the scene of international politics.*

Since this description of the behavior of nations defines power as the instrument for the attainment of ends, both national and supranational, the question

* *Politics among the Nations,* pp. 25–26.

about the capacity of nations to be loyal to over-arching systems of culture and value still remains. Morgenthau raises the question more thoroughly in a chapter, "The Ideological Element in International Politics," * in which he describes the idealistic claims and pretensions of statesmen to loyalty to more inclusive values, most of which were disclosed by subsequent history to be fraudulent. He points to a record of pretension and hypocrisy which should dismay and discourage all naive idealists who know nothing about the moral ambiguity of political order, particularly on the international level. But one has the feeling that a further question should have been raised about this almost universal hypocrisy. That question is whether or not there is anything in the anatomy of man, as a "rational" and "moral" creature, which prompts his embarrassment about the consistent self-regard of his parochial community and the consequent hypocrisy of claiming a higher motive than the obvious one.

The answer to this question is the more important in analyzing Morgenthau's thought since he has a unique reason for emphasizing the "national interest" as a description of the most powerful collective motive and as the norm of conduct. But Morgen-

* *Ibid.*, pp. 80 ff.

thau, despite his critics, is not a proponent of arrogant nationalism. He is merely suggesting that it would be both honest and moral for nations to confess their real motives, rather than to pretend to have nobler ones.

If we analyze the anatomy of man as both a rational and a social creature, we may discover why there is always hypocrisy in human nature, and specifically in national attitudes. Man is, as has been established in every analysis of human nature, a social creature. He is also a rational one. His rational capacity enables him to extend his sense of social obligation to wider communities than the parochial and effectively organized national community. His reason also enables him to construct philosophical, political, religious, and scientific structures of culture and civilization wider than the parochial community of the nation. These supranational cultures and systems of value are obviously real. Men would like their nations to be loyal to these higher values. The nations may be loyal, but only to the point where the interests of the nation are not in conflict with the higher values. What would be more "natural" than that both citizens and nations should pretend a deeper and more sacrificial loyalty of the nation to the higher values (of communities) than historic nations have proved to be capable of realizing?

In short, the hypocrisy of nations, as of individuals, may be an index to a residual creative capacity of their freedom, neither equal to nor effaced by their stronger impulse of self-regard. Hypocrisy, which is the tribute paid by the less acceptable impulse to the more acceptable one, is certainly no virtue. On the other hand, its elimination by canceling out the higher loyalty offers no moral gain. Nazi nationalism was not more virtuous because it was brutally cynical in making national aggrandisement the only end in its hierarchy of values.

One suspects that in Morgenthau's realistic rigor to isolate the dominant motive of the nations from the pretended higher one, he may have made the mistake of obscuring the important residual creative factor in human rationality. This suspicion is supported by his description of the relation of the will-to-power to the impulse of love in human nature. He writes: "The lust for power is, as it were, the twin of despairing love. Power becomes a substitute for love. What man can not achieve for any length of time through love he tries to achieve through power; to fulfill himself, to make himself whole by overcoming his loneliness, his isolation." *

The relation between lust for power and love is

* Hans Morgenthau, *The Restoration of American Politics* (Chicago: University of Chicago Press, 1962), p. 10.

actually quite different. The parent's power impulse is not a substitute for, but a corruption of, the love impulse toward the child. The statesman's will to power is not a substitute for, but a corruption of, his desire to serve his community. This distinction is important; for if valid, it would point to the residual force, but not the effacement, of the higher, or wider, or nobler loyalty, however much corrupted by the lower one.

Although it is important to establish the fact that the strength of the modern nation's self-regard and power impulse has not eliminated the residual capacity of peoples and nations for loyalty to values, cultures, and civilizations of wider and higher scope than the interests of the nation, it is also obvious that the proportionate strength of the "lower" and the "higher" motives and ends is seriously altered in collective morality. It would therefore be inaccurate to speak of the nation's power impulse being a "corruption" of its higher loyalty, as is the case of the parent in the family and the statesman in the nation.

The power impulse of the nation is, in fact, so strong, and its sense of a higher loyalty so weak, that only an irrelevant idealism would speculate about the possibility of the nation subordinating its national interest to that of an overarching culture. The importance of establishing this residual creative freedom in collective man lies not in the possibility of subordinating the lower to the higher or wider interest—but in the possibility that even a residual loyalty to values, transcending national existence, may change radically the nation's conception of the breadth and quality of its "national interest."

The importance of this issue must become apparent in an analysis of the behavior of the two current "super-nations," Russia and America, who both have power of imperial proportions, though only Russia is the center of an imperial congerie of power. Both nations are hegemonous in this supranational culture or civilization. American culture is pluralistic, "Christian" in terms of tradition and democratic in terms of political ideals. It is usually briefly defined as "Western," which describes its original base in Europe, but does not comprehend all the nations of the world who are anxious to establish or preserve free institutions. The Marxist culture is more sharply defined and tightly organized. It is based on a revolutionary, utopian, religio-political dogma which promises redemption from all social evils through the abolition of property. It is a jealous creed, which scorns the pluralism of the West and intends to annihilate all cultural and scientific and religious interests and groups which do not subscribe to its dogma. Obviously the cultures to which the two hegemonous nations are loyal are quite disparate.

But the relations of the two nations to their respective cultures are strikingly similar. Both are in the hegemonous position through the strength of their continental economies and through the consequent ability to mount the ultimate nuclear weapons of an atomic age. The proportion of force in the compound of power is not new in the realm of international relations, although the destructive power of the military force has a novel dimension.

In both blocks and cultures there is no question about the capacity or inclination of the nation to subordinate its "national interest" to the interests of the culture. The ideological factor offers the point of concurrence between the parochial and the wider interest. The loyalty of the respective hegemonous nations to the ideological content of the culture is actually a source of prestige to them, and therefore a part of their compound of power. This point of concurrence between the parochial community and the overarching culture obviates the necessity of sacrificing one to the other, but it does transmute the content of the national interest.

The economic sacrifices of foreign aid to which both nations are increasingly committed are not really sacrifices in terms of national interest. They may, however, translate the national interest into terms of consideration of economic advantage, which then will satisfy the conscience of its most sensitive citizens.

Both nations are subject to the criticism that they use their hegemonous advantage for the sake of their own interests, and both are subject to this temptation. Both have recalcitrant allies, France and China, who are critical of the ideological loyalty or wisdom of the hegemonous nations. In each case, national frustration of a less powerful nation may prompt the change of internal or external policy to make the hegemonous nation a better or purer exemplar of a common faith or system of values. The effect of the concern for American prestige in the colored world upon America's domestic race attitudes is a striking example of the creative influence of the responsibilities of hegemony.

This dialectic relation between the values of a culture and the self-regard of the hegemonous nations reveals that the national interest cannot be simply defined. All the elements of prestige, power, and force must be accounted for. In that case, the complexity of the relation would refute both realistic and idealistic interpretations of national behavior, although in essential accord with a moderate realism. The important issue of such an analysis is that a web of mutual and universal or general interests is discovered in which the national interests are inextricably related, so that a narrow definition of the interest of the nation would lead to the defeat of that interest. It would be merely a vivid reminder that the

morality of collective man in its highest reaches is
governed by a wise apprehension of concurrent interests, rather than by a sacrifice of the "lower" to
the "higher" interests. This prudence is a modest
but important triumph of human reason and sympathy over the tribal parochialism in human nature,
which is a symbol of the limits of freedom in the
creature who is bound to nature even while he becomes a creator in history.

The cold war and the precarious nuclear peace between the two contestants and their respective hegemonous nations vividly illustrates the important but
limited freedom of collective man. The contest is
between two cultures and civilizations. Cultures as
such have a survival impulse but no will-to-power.
Only the Communist culture is politically organized,
and its creed prompts a revolutionary grasp for
power. It has therefore been quite legitimately ac-
cused of seeking world domination, although that
accusation could be made against any culture, and
was made against the seventh-century Islamic movement, which assumed that its credo would find world
acceptance through persuasion and through the
force of arms.

Cultures are more universal than integral nations,
and thus more obviously fruits of the human imagination, rather than artifacts of political and or-

ganizing contrivance. Both cultures claim ideals of universal validity. The democratic ideals may be universally valid but not universally attainable, since their realization requires skills and competence which are not easily universalized either within the separate nations or among the nations of the world. The Communist ideal claims to have a remedy for all social evils; but its utopian ideals are prompted by the highly contingent circumstances of early European industrialism. Since the open societies of the West have eliminated the injustices of early industrialism by their own democratic, and not by Communist, means, the Communist scheme of redemption has little relevance for precisely the "capitalistic-democratic" culture for which it was designed.

The contrasting cultures are, in short, universal in intention but not in the power of realization. They consequently divide the world; and a precarious peace is observed between them only because the respective hegemonous nations each have nuclear power of such destructive capacity to threaten the other with virtual annihilation, but which gives no defense against its own destruction.

Thus a precarious nuclear peace, based on a "balance of terror," has been established in the world because the novel dimension of destructive capacity in nuclear weapons creates an identity between mutual interest and self-interest in the two contestants. Each lacks the capacity or inclination to sacrifice its own interests for the good of mankind, since such a sacrifice would mean capitulation to the adversary. Both lack sufficient mutual trust to engage in a large-scale partnership of peace. But the ideological chasm between them has been bridged by their common sense of responsibility for avoiding nuclear catastrophe. The recently negotiated limited test-ban agreement may be the first step in politically acknowledging this common responsibility.

Thus finally the interests of the community of mankind are obliquely served by the concern of both contestants for their own survival. This universal community—the dream of Hebraic Messianism and Stoic universalism, the concern of idealists from Augustine and Dante to the French utopians—although not sufficiently organized to become the concern of practical statecraft, is brought into historical calculations and indirect concerns.

That it should be only an indirect concern is a validation of the realistic theory of the limited character of human freedom. That even an indirect concern should require a prudent calculation of the concurrence of partial and general interests is a validation of all theories which emphasize the importance of residual freedom of human rationality. Man indeed is always the creator and agent in history; but this final predicament reveals that his creative freedom is limited to the limits of man as creature.

This final ironic culmination of the dreams of the ages for the fulfillment of a universal community, consonant with the obvious universality of the human spirit, reveals the whole scope of the relation of human nature, with its finite and indeterminate dimensions of human freedom, to the organization of human communities. They are always more limited than the projects of human imagination. They reveal that, while man may be universal as free spirit, he is always parochial and tribal in the achievement of organized community. Thus we are witnessing a final revelation of the incongruity of human existence.

MAN'S TRIBALISM
AS ONE SOURCE
OF HIS INHUMANITY

HUMAN BEINGS are capable of treating their fellowmen with both cruelty and kindness in all their relations. Family relations are usually based on mutual love, but cruel parents are by no means rare. Yet the chief source of man's inhumanity to man seems to be the tribal limits of his sense of obligation to other men.

At this very moment in history, cruelties aggravated by human tribalism occupy the news and preoccupy our minds. America, which has prided itself on being the "melting pot" of many ethnic groups, is, with great difficulty, trying to erase the last remnant of slavery a century after the Civil War. All over the world, there are struggles where new nations are being born, inevitably accompanied by these same inhumanities.

In the budding nation on the island of Cyprus, Greek and Turkish compatriots are murdering each other. Remnants of former empires, they are incapable of establishing either a common citizenship or a common humanity. Race is not the only mark of tribalism, although it is usually predominant. In the new nation of South Vietnam, the mutual enmity between Buddhist majority and Catholic minority makes a common community impossible. Any distinguishing mark between the "we group," in which mutual responsibilities are acknowledged, and a "they group," who are outside the pale of humanity, may serve the tribal character of human nature. The distinguishing marks of tribalism may consist of common racial origins, or language, or religion and culture, or class.

Language is usually the most obvious source of tribal identification, but it is more malleable than race. The invention of printing served in European culture to enlarge the tribe to nation by giving victory to the printed language over the vocally transmitted dialects of sub-national racial groups. It also enabled the budding nations of Europe to gain political autonomy over the empires, who had no common language but whose élite spoke a semi-universal language (Latin). These autonomous nations sometimes created a common language powerful enough to absorb racial minorities, as the Celtic minorities in the multi-racial United Kingdom of Great Britain, and even all the tongues of European immigrants in the English-speaking multi-racial United States.

Meanwhile the fierce and brutal tribal conflicts in the Congo reveal that the primitive culture has not yet achieved a common language, necessary to subdue sub-national tribalism. Even the largest and most impressive African nation, Nigeria, has revealed its regional difficulties, to which both tribal dialects and diverse religious traditions—Islamic, Christian, and animistic—contribute.

The tribal cruelties in mid-twentieth-century news are of two types. One, of which the Cyprus cruelties are typical, consists merely of brutal warfare between two groups in a parochial community. The second type consists of cruelties of oppression practiced by a politically powerful racial group against an impotent and helpless racial majority (as in South Africa), or against a racial and religious minority (as in Nazi Germany), or against a racial minority of such large proportions that the racial "white" majority feels its political monopoly of power to be threatened (as in the state of Mississippi).

It may be significant that the brutalities of open conflict are spiritually less debasing than the enslavement of one tribal group by another. The brutalities of tyranny, whether in Nazi Germany or in South Africa or in Mississippi, are more wounding to human self-esteem than any conflict.

Class distinctions without racial, religious or linguistic distinctions have never been too severe since the rise of modern technical and democratic cultures. They were, of course, the cause of ages of brutal oppression in the long night of ancient and medieval cultures in which the distinction between landowners and landless and impotent peasants raised all kinds of barriers to the recognition of an obvious common humanity.

The Marxist dogma arose from the historical situation in the beginning of early nineteenth-century industrialism. For it was then that the development of the machine transferred the skill and the tool of the craftsman to the domain and the power of the owners. Thus both "labor" as well as the machines became the "commodity" of the owners. The middle classes, for the time being, aggravated the inequalities of the earlier feudalism. Thus Marx, the first prophet of the new political religion, plausibly could portray the bourgeoisie as the ultimate devils in the drama of history, who would aggravate social brutalities until a suffering mankind would in desperation "expropriate the expropriators" and usher in a classless and just society. The bourgeoisie did not prove to be the devils of history; but neither were they saints. A century was needed before a free society could refute their bourgeois ideology. In the process, it also refuted the Marxist apocalypse and perfected the political and the economic instruments of justice in the political and economic sphere, and thereby proved that economic power was not the only form of social power and that property ownership was not the only form of economic power. In short, Western open and technical cultures refuted the political religion specifically designed for them and became immune to the Marxist virus of rebellion. Unfortunately the apocalypse was more relevant to non-technical cultures in the last stages of agrarian feudalism, which were suffering from the expansive impulses of the technically powerful West. There its gospel of anti-imperialism proved politically potent.

In a democratic and technically competent culture the marks of class are infinitely varied but never indelible. Class interests are thus the cause of complex economic and political rivalries but are seldom the source of inhuman brutalities. If the racial factor in the component of class is dominant, however, the indignities of class domination frequently tend to inhuman brutality. Thus the caste system of ancient India was first created by the distinction between the Aryan priest and soldier invaders of the subcontinent, and the local, dark-skinned lower castes. Religions elaborated vocational distinctions to absurd length.

In Latin America, the racial component in the class system, furnished by the Spanish conquerors as landlords and the Indian population as serfs, gave European feudalism the strength to outlast the medieval culture and to complicate the problems of introducing both technical efficiency and democratic institutions in the southern hemisphere.

Of course America had its great task in eliminating the last vestiges of slavery a century after the slaves were ostensibly freed. The struggle shows how class brutalities are aggravated through racial distinction. The Negro minority in the United States suffers not only because its darker skin is such an obvious mark of race and class identity but because slavery has left its evil heritage of social contempt for the former slave race, as well as a cultural backwardness only transcended by the most gifted members of the race. Therefore American Negro citizens are the only genuine proletarians in a bourgeois paradise; and only the most consistent political pressure will redeem the Negroes of the Deep South from the brutalities of the white oligarchy, and Negroes everywhere from the social odium that is an offense both to their humanity and to their rights as citizens of the nation.

America's difficulties with this racial minority,

with such an unhappy past of "previous condition of servitude," is the more striking since the country had no difficulty in absorbing most of the European immigrants, who furnished the sinews of its growing industrial power in the nineteenth century. An established common language and dispersion of the immigrant groups over a whole continent hastened the absorption. A common language did not help the Negro group, nor, for that matter, a common Protestant faith with the dominant white majority. The hazards of an obvious "color" mark of race and of historically contingent cultural backwardness were insurmountable.

The difficulties America has experienced in acknowledging the common humanity with a racial minority marked by observable racial identification of dark color and by historically caused cultural backwardness give us a vivid example of the basic paradox of man's inhumanity to man. That paradox consists, on the one hand, in the obvious unity and common humanity of men, derived from their rational freedom over nature and the indeterminate creative possibilities of that freedom, which distinguishes them from other animals and constitutes the human race as one single species. It consists, on the other hand, in the fact that this supposedly rational creature is able to recognize a common humanity only in the uncommon and unique marks of a tribal "we group," which therefore come to be the basis of all parochial—or more recently, "national"—communities in which the dignity of man is respected and rights are acknowledged and enforced; while others, lacking these obvious marks of tribal identity, whether racial, linguistic, cultural, or religious, are treated brutally as if they were not part of a common human race.

The Greek and Roman Stoics were the first consistent proponents of the common humanity of man. Unfortunately they regarded human parochialism and tribalism as a remedial error which could be corrected by reason. Let us consider the statement of the Stoic creed made by Cicero, Roman philosopher and universalistic ideal of the whole of Western civilization: *

> Out of all the material of the philosophers' discussions, surely there comes nothing more valuable than the full realization that we are born to justice, and that right is based, not upon men's opinion, but upon nature. This fact will immediately be plain if you once get a clear conception of Man's fellowship and union with his fellowmen. For no single thing is so like another, so exactly its counterpart, as all of us are to one another. Nay, if

* Cicero, *De Legibus,* I, x, 28–31.

bad habits and false beliefs did not twist the weaker minds, and turn them into whatever direction they are inclined, no one would be so like his own self as all men would be like all others.

And so, however we may define man, a single definition will apply to all. This is a sufficient proof that there is no difference in kind between man and man; For if there were, one definition would not be applicable to all men. And indeed, the reason, which alone raises us above the beasts, and enables us to draw inferences, to prove and disprove, to discuss problems and to come to conclusions, is certainly common to us all, and though in varying in what it learns, at least in the capacity to learn it is invariable. . . . The similarity in the human race is as clearly marked in its evil as well as in its goodness. For pleasure also attracts all men; and even though it is an enticement to vice, yet it has some likeness to what is naturally good.

The tremendous achievement of universalist humanism was one consequence of this peculiar metaphysical interpretation of history. Another result, more dubious as well as partly erroneous, was the obscuring of all natural and historical distinctions between man and man. According to the Stoics, these distinctions were apparent or accidental and were due to "false opinion." But they are real enough to have been the cause of all parochial communities of history and of all inhuman brutalities in the conflict between these human communities that tend to deny the common humanity of the adversary. The common humanity is obvious; but the distinguishing marks which separate man from man are also more obvious, more persistent, and more general than the classical universalists realized.

Subsequent history and more particularly modern anthropological sciences therefore validated Stoic universalism, for evidence multiplied that the uniquely human qualities, which the Stoics defined as "reason," comprehended capacities to transcend natural limitations in indeterminate degree. Cicero was right in saying that the degree of freedom varied with learning, but that "the capacity to learn is invariable." Thus the unique human freedom which distinguishes men from brutes was and is truly the basis of a common humanity and of a potential sense of kinship with all men.

But, on the other hand, the whole of history revealed that even the most learned men would not be rational enough to penetrate and transform the unconscious and sub-rational sources of parochial loyalties, which determine the limits of community and which prompt inhuman brutalities to other human beings, who do not share the same marks of race, language, religion, or culture. All historians and political scientists have accepted the curious paradox lying at the heart of human universalist aspirations and at the same time making history the tangled story of endless forms of community and communal conflict. For man is inclined to accept mutual responsibilities for the preservation of "life, liberty, and the pursuit of happiness" only in limited communities, and in those defined by the unique marks of racial and tribal distinction, which clearly violate and obscure the common humanity of man. The Stoics were right in asserting the common humanity of man, and wrong in underestimating the power and persistence of tribalism in human history.

Western culture was strongly influenced by Stoic universalism because early Christianity incorporated many of its ethical categories. The early church also inherited from the Hebrew prophets an implicit universalism which had existed side by side with the concept of the "chosen people." St. Paul, according to the Book of Acts, preached in Athens in an idiom which would have been understood by Jew or Greek: God "made from one every nation of men to live on all the face of the earth . . . " (ACTS 17:26); and "There is neither Jew nor Greek; there is neither slave nor free, there is neither male nor female; for you are all one in Christ Jesus" (GALATIANS 3:28). Unfortunately, the incorporation of universalism into a specific religion inadvertently set up a new mark

94

of tribal distinction; and Christian universalism did not save the Jews, who remained loyal to the old faith, from the brutalities of Christian anti-Semitism with its awful pogroms against the Jewish heretics.

Nor did a common Christian faith save the Negro minority in America because the racial identification was too obvious, and the cultural distinctions due to slavery too obtrusive. A high degree of cultural sophistication is in fact necessary to reveal that cultural and religious marks of identification are historically contingent. It must have been as difficult for the civilized Romans to discover a common humanity with the barbarian European hordes who overran the empire as for modern white oligarchies in Africa and America to recognize that cultural differences between Negro and white groups are not innate but historically contingent.

No one could deny that cultural and moral differences between groups and nations are real. But only time and experience will prove that they are not innate, and that in any case they cannot reasonably deny a common humanity in all men. The modern British are more successful in maintaining parliamentary democracy than most of the Continental nations, not because of an innate political wisdom in the British character, but because of a whole series of contingencies in the European conflict between the feudalism of the Middle Ages and modern open societies. If modern Negro minorities are more gifted in the arts and in acquiring the legal and other learning than they are in the spirit of "enterprise," that too may be due to past history in the cultural traditions of their race.

Marks of racial distinction are, of course, more indelible and "natural." But we have previously noted that a common language, more malleable than physical factors, has the capacity to transmute the sense of a common racial kinship, either extending or contracting the sense of kinship. Centuries may be required to change the sense of racial kinship of African tribal primitivism to something similar to the European sense of national kinship. On the whole, language extends the boundaries of race under a technical culture. But it may also contract it. Thus the invention of printing and the simultaneous translation of the Bible changed the vaguely defined northern region, outside the medieval empire and under Danish sovereignty, into three distinct Scandinavian "nations"—Denmark, Sweden, and Norway.

But the same set of historical contingencies gave the German tribes one language, while the Scandinavians developed three. But various cultural, religious, and political factors prevented this single "nation" from achieving political unification until Bismarck accomplished the task by "blood and iron" in the late nineteenth century. Thus human history presents us with a bewildering series of multiple causations, natural and contrived, which serve to reveal that the Stoic and subsequently the medieval distinction between "nature" and history was much too simple. Perhaps it would be more correct to affirm that the classical identification of the historical with the natural was mistaken.

Augustine, in *De Civitate Dei,* made sport of Cicero's optimism in asserting that the Roman empire was built on a "compact of justice," and pointed out that its cement of cohesion was in fact the power of the Roman military might; and that men who spoke different languages did not in fact acknowledge their universal human kinship; but rather they hated each other. However, Augustine's "realism" was too excessive to do justice to the Roman and Stoic genius for universal community or, rather, for the quasi-universal imperial community. He aggravated this error by a fantastic distinction, drawn from Neo-Platonism—the distinction between the "city of this world," presumably the political realm, and the "city of God," presumably although not definitely the church. In the one "the love of self and the contempt of God" ruled; while in the other "the love of God and contempt of the self" prevailed. Naturally, the more obvious obligation to love the neighbor as the self, which is the genuine part of Christian universalism, was obscured by this neo-Platonic division between the "two cities." It is only fair to observe, however, that the Catholic tradition has preserved a trans-national and trans-racial universalism more successfully than Protestantism which, together with Eastern Catholic Orthodoxy, became the ally of the budding nation-states. The universalist tradition of medieval culture was so strong that Dante in *De Monarchia* tried in the late medieval period to justify this universalism against papal absolutism.

Dante made his nostalgic effort to recreate the Roman and the medieval empires before the rise of the nation-states. These emerging nations, with their own ethnic and linguistic cores of homogeneity, seemed to put an end to the Stoic, Christian, and Hebraic ideal of a universal humanity which transcends all tribal loyalties. The French Enlightenment restored the Stoic ideal with its slogan of the "rights of man," and also committed afresh the Stoic error of assuming that those rights would be easily recognized and self-enforcing. The French Revolution, with its Bonapartist aftermath of French nationalism, seemed to be an ironic death of a dream. The rights of man were swallowed up in the rights of a newly self-conscious nation.

The rise of nations in the modern or post-medieval period first had fragmented the ostensible universal community of the papal medieval empire. Tribalism and particularism thus seemed to triumph over the rights of man as man existing in a universal moral system of mutual obligation and of the recognition and respect for human beings as members of the same race, endowed with dignity and transcending brute creation. But this is not the final chapter.

The final chapter is now being written in those democratic nations which have digested most forms of ethnic, linguistic, and cultural pluralism, and which have laws formulating human rights. But these human rights, however morally attractive, are not self-enforcing. Their enforcement demands the assertion of political authority by the politically and culturally integrated community, thereby insuring human rights for all its citizens. The modern liberal democratic nation-state thus furnishes the climax of the paradox of man's tribalism and his universalism.

This final chapter for the United States is the story of the civil rights controversy. The nation, reluctant so long, now at last shows its intention and resolve to establish the human rights of its Negro minority.

This whole movement shows how glaring was the contradiction involved in the "American Dilemma." The Declaration of Independence declared, and the

Bill of Rights of the Constitution guaranteed, human rights to all American citizens. Yet many of those citizens whose slave-forefathers were emancipated in the Civil War are deprived of the very rights affirmed in American political tradition and assumed as universal in American culture.

Why were more than a century and a revolution of the deprived humanity needed to challenge this contradiction between profession or promise and the fact of deprivation of human rights? Perhaps a re-examination of some of the issues of the Civil War may suggest a clue both to the tardiness of the nation in overcoming this contradiction and in justifying the hope that finally the "American Dilemma" will be resolved.

The coming of the Civil War showed again that a nation is neither able nor willing to enforce universal human rights until its own self-interest, that is, the interest of the whole nation, is involved. The Civil War lesson is the more impressive because the "saviour" of a divided nation, Abraham Lincoln, though a Jeffersonian idealist who did not believe in slavery, nevertheless confessed that "my primary interest is to save the Union." That is to say, he placed the preservation of the nation in a primary position in his scale of values; and the emancipation of slaves was ordered merely as a war measure to insure the victory of the Union forces against the rebellion. The actual proclamation may have exhibited, as a learned historian observed, "all the eloquence of a bill of lading." In any case, the freed slaves were not given the economic resources of free citizenship; though, fortunately, the moral content of the abolition movement inspired many efforts to give an education to this deprived minority.

The tribal prejudice against the Negro was so potent because that minority suffered from the onus of its "previous condition of servitude," its lack of technical and cultural competence, and its dark skin, diverging too obviously from the dominant white type. It naturally took some time for the gifted members of the race to offer irrefutable proof that these deficiencies were not due to "innate" inferiorities, and that the proposition of a common and universal humanity was in no way refuted. It also required some time for the more fortunate and enterprising members of the race to acquire an education, since both the right to vote (political power) and the right to be educated (cultural power) were denied to members of the minority, primarily but not solely in the old slave states in which white oligarchies tried to preserve the political and economic advantage of the slave system.

It is not our purpose, and beyond our competence,

to trace the devious political factors which entered into the connivance of the white majority in both parties and in both the North and the South to perpetuate these various forms of disfranchisement. Dean Griswold of the Harvard Law School has given an account of this dismal chapter of our national life, verse by verse, in his volume *Law and Lawyers in the United States,** particularly in his chapter five entitled "Slavery and the Common Law." This sad record of our national life includes, of course, the defiance of post-Civil War constitutional amendments specifically designed to assure all citizens "equal protection of the laws."

The part played by the national interest in the emancipation of the Negro minority is important. Yet, to avoid undue cynicism in emphasizing this, other contributions must be remembered. The decision of the Supreme Court in 1954 in outlawing segregated schools not only contributed the "majesty of law" to this emancipation but actually initiated the first step in the Negro revolt. For it transmuted the desperation of the minority into that wonderful combination of hope and despair, which has been the motive power of all rebellions against injustice.

Also noteworthy was the leadership given to this

---

* Harvard University Press, 1964.

revolution by Negro members of the professions and of the arts, as well as by Negro students. Their outstanding contribution was evidence of universal humanity, as well as of the historical and contingent character of inequality, regarded as innate by the racists. It was the brief of a Negro lawyer, Thurgood Marshall, which persuaded the Supreme Court to make its historic decision. The artistic gifts of Negro actors, writers, and musicians meanwhile recall the way that the artists and craftsmen of the late medieval period articulated the hopes and fears of the inarticulate peasant masses.

The contributions of the religious communities varied in quality and degree, although the obligation of universal human rights was explicit in all their creeds. The Catholic Church supported desegregation, at least in its official pronouncements and in the racial integration of its parochial schools. The Jews were prompted by their laws and traditions to benevolence and concern for an underprivileged group.

The witness of Protestantism, generally speaking, too often was sadly lacking. The kind of Protestantism in the old slave states was an individualistic, evangelistic perfectionism. It was congregational in character and polity, and it lacked association with the broadly based community of the Christian church. Southern evangelistic Christianity almost universally was dominated by the mores and viewpoint of its congregation. Thus neither the congregation, usually under the aegis of a White Citizens' Council, nor the traditional emphasis on individual conversion could root out social evil of long standing. Fortunately, the consensus of white Protestant churches of all denominations throughout the nation gave support to the civil rights movement in its final stages. But these supports from the religious communities, though tardily but sincerely given, were obviously not enough to engage the whole nation in the difficult task of protecting the human rights of its deprived minority, if the national interest of the whole nation had not been obviously engaged in the task.

The fact that the interest of the whole nation is involved in this struggle for human rights is shown vividly in the following ways. First, it is in the national interest of a free nation to have the harmony which only justice can guarantee. For a revolutionary racial minority endangers the harmony of a democratic society in the same way as did the industrial workers of the nineteenth century, proving in this loyal revolt that a free society has resources which the Marxists had miscalculated. Secondly, an increasing technical culture needs trained manpower. Thus untrained workers do not serve the national interest. Hence the retraining program of the federal government and also its anti-poverty program are clearly inspired, at least in part, by the nation's concern for its economic advantages. Finally, world opinion, especially in this day of mass communication, is important for American power and prestige. The rise of new nations in Asia and Africa relates our solution of this domestic problem to our moral prestige abroad. Thus the national interest is involved.

Needless to say, none of these national concerns can be defined as purely "moral." But we should have come at last to the conclusion that the paradox of man's tribal and universal nature must exhibit, and be solved by, the most diverse resources in his nature.

The harnessing of the national interest to the project of guarding these human rights and liberties will not assure necessarily a quick triumph of the enterprise. The historical tribal roots of prejudice have too long accumulated, and the marks of racial distinction are too obvious to guarantee the triumph over them, even by a united and powerful national government which speaks and acts for a new national consensus.

All that may be said is that the beginning of the project has been propitious, and that the problem will probably concern the nation for at least a century, even as the tolerable solution of the problem of economic justice required the resources of democracy throughout the nineteenth century.

MAN'S SELFHOOD

IN ITS SELF-SEEKING

AND SELF-GIVING

MAN'S self-seeking and self-giving are intricately related in the human self. Human freedom makes for a unique and dialectical relation of the individual to the community. On the one hand, it transmutes nature's instinct for survival into a variety of forms of self-realization, including vanity, the will-to-power and the desire for a full selfhood, which must include always relations to neighbors and communities. On the other hand, the freedom of the self gives man an infinite variety of relationships with his community, from social dependence to social creativity. Thus man's selfhood is involved in an intricate relation of self-seeking and self-giving. The paradoxical observation of Jesus about this relation is accurate. He said, "He who finds his life will lose it, and he who loses his life for my sake will find it." This aphorism might be interpreted as follows: consistent self-seeking is bound to be self-defeating; on the other hand, self-giving is bound to contribute ultimately to self-realization.

The social substance of human existence makes this paradoxical relation inevitable. The community, chiefly the family in the infancy of the self, is the primary source of the self's security which enables the self to love and relate its life to others. The psychoanalytic study of the child has shown how the security of the self is derived from the love it experienced in childhood from "the mothering one." On the other hand, the family and a whole complex of communities are the arena in which the self, freed of undue self-concern, is able to relate itself to others. first in parental affection and responsibility to the children and to the mate in the family, which continues to be the most primary, as it is the most primordial, of all human communities.

Thus the gift of security given by parents to children is transmuted naturally into the ability of even those parents, who are otherwise self-seeking, to be "self-giving" in their relations to their family. Thus modern psychiatry has validated and given new emphasis to what was defined in orthodox religious thought as "common grace." This element of "grace" may be defined as the "gift" of security, without which the self is incapable of becoming free of preoccupation with its own security so that it might relate itself to others and achieve true fulfill-ment of the self.*

Naturally, in civilized communities, the family is not the only community through which the self is made secure and in turn is offered the opportunity of self-fulfillment through self-giving. These other communities include not only the various civic com-munities, from tribe to city-state, to empire and na-tion. They also include all communities of culture which engage creatively the reason and imagination of the self, thus leading to self-realization by the ful-fillment of all its talents.

All this does not change the basic fact that self-seeking, practiced too consistently without regard to the social substance of self-fulfillment, must be self-defeating. Nor do all the achievements of civilized life alter the other part of the paradox, namely that the capacity of the self to relate itself to others cannot be achieved by a robust moral will. It is a gift of the

* The word "grace" is a translation of the Greek *charis* and the Latin *gratias*. Its original meaning is therefore a free gift, not a reward for merit. The theological usage of the word frequently obscures the original meaning, but it is reflected in such general usage of the meaning of gift, in the words "gracious" or "graceful" in which the freedom of the gift is emphasized. "Grateful" is obviously meant to designate the response to a free gift.

original security of the self; that is, it is a matter of "grace."

Erich Fromm in his *Man for Himself,* as also others, defines the capacity to love as a "phenomenon of abundance," but mistakenly he assumes that the abundance of security which enables the self to love is derived from its previous self-seeking. It is more correct to regard the abundance of security as furnished by the love and devotion which others give the self, as Erik Erikson, for example, illustrates with his concept of "basic trust." * Thus we have a complete circle of the paradox: consistent self-seeking is self-defeating; but self-giving is impossible to the self without resources furnished by the community, in the first instance, the family.

Thus modern empirical studies support the paradox of Jesus. But there are two aspects of the intricate relation between self-seeking and self-giving which have been confused, rather than illuminated, by orthodox doctrine, both Catholic and Reformation. The first is the confusion pertaining to the theological distinction between "common grace" and "saving grace." This distinction is valid only insofar as

* Erik H. Erikson, *Childhood and Society,* 2nd edition (New York: W. W. Norton, 1963).
See also: *Insight and Responsibilities* (New York: W. W. Norton, 1964), esp. "Human Strength and the Cycle of Generations," pp. 115 ff.

the community of faith or the religious tradition is able to supply an additional resource for freeing the self from idolatrous forms of communal loyalties. By definition and tradition, "saving grace" is induced by a religious experience in which the conscience of the individual self transfers devotion from a contingent community, such as family, race or nation, to an ultimate loyalty to God, the fountainhead of the whole realm of value.

Actually the force of "saving grace" has a different course in history than the one marked out for it according to the theory. It has emphasized the loyalty of individuals to the immediate community, rather than emancipating them from idolatrous worship of common loyalties. Thus loyalty to religious faith and to its ethical traditions has affected the standards of fidelity in marriage, as are shown even in the statistics of the Kinsey report. But the religious commitment in itself does not necessarily make the family, the community of loyal individuals, for example, responsible for the well-being of other families. The family as family cannot detach itself from its own self-interest to seek actively the well-being of other families.

In the community of faith—the church or the denomination—this domestication of love is shown not only passively in lack of concern but also positively in the sins of religious fanaticism and bigotry.

Ideally the church is a community of "saved" individuals, who know themselves to be "forgiven sinners." This ideal should make for humility; but the long history of religious self-righteousness reveals that religious experience is more effective in inducing repentance for deviation from common standards than in inducing repentance for the hatred, bigotry, and prejudice involved in the common standards of race and nation, or church. The adherent of religion must come to terms with the historic facts, that in all collective behavior religious piety is likely to sanctify historical and contingent viewpoints. Historically speaking, religious piety is more apt to be found claiming the divine for an ally of its own partial viewpoints—"It has seemed good to the Holy Spirit and to us"—rather than showing a humble awareness of the relative aspects of all historical loyalties or as bringing forth the fruits of repentance for shortcomings as judged by the transcendent God.

All this is a human rather than a peculiarly or uniquely religious phenomenon. Both the French and the Russian revolution showed it was easy to do this without benefit of clergy. Thus it was the curious quirks of the collective self which prompted all men to claim ultimate validity for contingent collective values. In both Jacobin and communist fanaticism, "truth" or "reason" or "Marxist-Leninist science" was worshipped as an absolute. Perhaps human selfhood in its collective form constitutionally is unable to imagine any higher value than the common value of its devotion. Hence, the redemptive value of dissident individuals, the prophet, the critic, even the rebel, in a free community.

Orthodox religious doctrine in a second way has confused this basic paradox of self-giving, self-striving and self-fulfilling. It has assumed that it is possible to suppress self-regard and to make the self unselfish and disinterested. This perfectionist hope is expressed in Catholicism particularly in its ascetic tradition and theology. In Protestantism it is found both in the Lutheran doctrine of the "heavenly realm" and in various perfectionist Protestant sects as also more generally in Protestant moralism.

This belief in perfectability has given the religious community too often the aura of self-righteousness. Religious people were ostensibly more "unselfish" than other mortals, although common experience refuted this pretension. Another consequence of this belief in perfectability was that all forms of self-regard and self-realization were denigrated and regarded as "sinful." Thus the truth in Jesus' original paradox was obscured. He had observed merely that a consistent desire for self-fulfillment was self-defeating. This is true because the self needs other selves in order to be itself. This is the nature of the self, and also is its destiny.

Christian thought also has obscured the provisional and relative merits of the ambitions of vital men, which well may contribute to their creativity in the community and in all the arts of civilization.

It would be impossible to trace the biographies of creative men to show that the push of ambition may have at least the provisional relation to the pull of their creative responsibilities because it furnishes them with an arena where these creative responsibilities take hold. But a cursory glance at the biographies of two great statesmen of the English-speaking world, Abraham Lincoln in the nineteenth century and Winston Churchill in the twentieth, illustrates this relation of ambition to creativity.

Lincoln's partner and biographer, Herndon, described Lincoln as a "very ambitious young man." His ambition prompted him to secure an education beyond the formal limits of his family. It persuaded him to apprentice in the law, to run for Congress, and finally to debate with Douglas on the slavery issue. All these ambitions did not, of course, necessarily involve the final destiny of his life, the Presidency of the nation. That goal was clearly beyond the limits of his imagination.

Ambition may not have been responsible for his native endowments or for his sense of style in rhetoric of which his Gettysburg Address and his Second

Inaugural Address were such striking examples. It did not endow him with that unique combination of a moderate anti-slavery impulse and a strong sense of national patriotism, tinged with a sense of mission for the preservation of a unique nation "so conceived and so dedicated," which made him prevail politically against his foes to gain the Presidency, and which also enabled him to be a resolute leader of an imperiled nation. Nor could ambition be held responsible for his spirit of charity, expressed in words, "With malice toward none, with charity for all, let us strive to do the work we are in." The drive and push of ambition may prompt young people to sharpen their talents and to furnish their minds with useful and creative stuff. It does not, of itself, create or recreate character. That original endowment, furnished by heritage and nature, may be used by the ambitious self in different ways. Both character and talent may give ambition scope and justification. "Vulgar ambition" is usually a drive disproportionate to talent, character, or occasion. Many men in our history were ambitious to be President of the nation—in Lincoln's day, for instance, William E. Seward, who seemed to have more justification than Lincoln, and Salmon Chase, who obviously had neither the talent nor the character to warrant his ambition. Thus ambition may be pathetic, when it is disproportionate to talent or character. Or it may be tragic if it is frustrated by devotion to a larger loyalty. The frequency of these tragic encounters between ambition and sacrificial loyalty to a cause which transcends the self is evidence for the fact that the relation between the push of ambition and the pull of a creative loyalty is not uniform but may be endlessly varied. Sometimes the ambition of a talented man may be frustrated by a pathetic flaw in an otherwise upright character.

To turn to another great exemplar of the relation of ambition to creativity, Winston Churchill, as the descendant of the famous first Duke of Marlborough, obviously started on a different rung of the ladder of success. While Churchill did not, any more than Lincoln, aspire to the exalted place he was to achieve in the annals of his nation, he was by all accounts a very ambitious young man. In fact, he was so obviously ambitious that when in the first World War the venture against the Turks at Gallipoli failed, his critics and enemies hailed the opportunity to cast him from the Cabinet. They revelled in the opportunity to cut down a very self-confident and ambitious young politician.

Yet Churchill's long stay in the political wilderness between the two world wars revealed that his ambition was not consistent enough to prevent loyalty to principle and policies which he held dear. When the opportunity came to put his unique talents in the service of the nation, it was not ambition but historical destiny which satisfied his craving for renown. In the day of success, his magnanimity toward his foes—Chamberlain, for instance—was the fruit of his own peculiar endowment on the one hand, but on the other it was made possible by the security which he had won.

Obviously the correlation between the push of ambition, the pull of creative loyalties, affections, and responsibilities, the innate character and the native or acquired talent, is never exact. Sometimes it is uncorrelated, for sometimes the strength of ambition pathetically is stronger than the native talent or character which would justify it. In the face of the varied evidence, all that can be said is that ambition or self-regard is not necessarily opposed to creativity, that sometimes it is the source of the push which gives the opportunity for the exercise of creativity.

The obvious fact that creative men who were known chiefly for their ambition in their youth proved themselves responsible, magnanimous, and generally virtuous in their maturity might be regarded cynically as a revelation of the virtues of maturity over youth. More profoundly, it should be regarded as the fruit of what the theologians call

"common grace," for ambition provided the particular niche and eminence in the social and cultural
structure in which they exercised their creativity.
But the pull of responsibility and the joy of exercis-
ing innate creative potentialities proved the efficacy
of the "pull" of common grace, the power of responsibilities and affections to draw the self beyond
itself, and thus create the condition for self-fulfillment which a consistent drive for self-realization can
not accomplish and which always leads to self-defeat.

The philosophies of self-abnegation, chiefly expressed in the ascetic tradition of all religions but
more particularly in the Christian and Buddhist faith,
reveal that it is as impossible to deny the self by any
act of the will or any discipline as to realize the self
by direct assertion of the self. The long ages of
ascetic and monastic culture, including the asceticism of medieval Christianity, show that only in rare
instances, as in St. Francis of Assisi, for instance, has
a lyrical and ecstatic note of self-denial been reached.
Usually the desire for prestige in a culture which
cherished self-denial was the hidden and perhaps unconscious motive of the ascetic individual. When the
monks turned from introspection to responsible
leadership in the arts, architecture, agronomy, or education, they were subject to the usual temptations
of self-regard, the desire for gain, power, and pres-

tige, which assailed most men. If they withdrew from the world in order to deny the self, they became involved in a vicious circle of preoccupation with the ego in an effort to get rid of it or to suppress it. The effort to deny the self also too often produced that curious paradox of the moral life, the development of pride in the achieving of humility.

Absolute self-negation is impossible because the self is never in rational control of all the unconscious stirrings of selfhood. Absolute self-realization also is impossible because the self contracts rather than expands when consciously and consistently it seeks its own ends.

The evidence of biographical history points to the primacy of grace in saving the self from undue and destructive self-regard. But this element of truth in the Pauline and Augustinian doctrines of grace must not obscure the fact that orthodox Christianity partially veiled what it sought to clarify by an undue emphasis on the distinction between "saving grace" and "common grace." The former meant an ultimate redemption from self-regard by the infusion, sacramental or evangelical or experiential, of divine grace into the dynamics of human selfhood. This distinction implied the superiority of conscious striving for grace over unconscious forms of it. Thus grace mediated through the security of parental affection, or the self-forgetfulness prompted by a crisis, or the pull of the exercise of creative capacities or of responsibilities and loyalties to a cause greater than the self, all of which are the daily experiences of mankind, are minimized in favor of a "saving grace" mediated by the church and consciously sought by the believer. Sometimes it may even be claimed as a reward for believing certain propositions in a theological system. St. Paul said we "are saved by grace." But he added, "Through faith in Jesus Christ." The early Reformation protested in the name of grace against legalism. Yet by the seventeenth century this came to mean that we are saved not only "by faith" but by *true* faith." This meant "faith" as "belief," belief in the symbolic affirmations of Lutheranism, in short, belief in the Augsburg Confession.

The historical conceptions of saving grace became salvation through belief and even right belief. This made the religious conception of grace even more confusing than the ascetic effort to rid the self of egoism through moral striving. Yet it must be recognized that there are certain elements of truth in this concept of saving grace. Those elements of truth are revealed in genuine evangelical experience in which the self apprehends a larger system of loyalty and meaning than the common loyalties and commitments which are the stuff of common grace.

These loyalties may, and do frequently, contain idolatrous elements such as the worship of a class or
nation or state or a parochial system of values. After
all, the Nazi system of values with its extravagant
nationalism and racism had provisional elements of
common grace in it because it gave aimless people a
"cause" for which they could devote their lives; but
it was revealed as a demonic form of grace. It merely
substituted an exaggerated collective egoism for individual egoism and brought destruction upon the
world and on the nation.

Not every form of parochial loyalty and commitment is as extravagant and demonic as the Nazi
form. Ordinarily the social life of man, the source of
common grace, is ordered in a series of sometimes
concentric and sometimes overlapping and conflicting circles. In a highly developed culture, the complex web of loyalties is a source of discrimination and
discipline and a guard against extravagant forms of
parochial loyalties which may draw the individual
from his self-concern, but at the price of substituting
collective for individual self-regard.

This web of conflicting and overlapping loyalties
does not have the same emotional appeal which an
ultimate religious commitment has. In that sense,
the religious experience, consequent upon a commitment to God or to "God in Christ," is an aspect of

saving grace. But the proponents of religion as the sole source of salvation, conceiving this commitment to be a guarantee against all idolatry, that is, against any inordinate devotion to contingent values, scarcely measure the evidence in history that such an ultimate commitment may well be wedded to, and the veil for, a parochial loyalty. The endless variety of combinations between ostensibly universal religious experiences and the passions of race, class, and nation reveals that redemption through "saving grace" is not as neat as perfectionist forms of Christianity assume.

The history of evangelical Protestantism with its policy of inducing a violent conversion from old mediocrities and complexities to a new and simpler devotion to God is as spotted as any historical movement. If we confine ourselves to America alone, we can trace the history of evangelical evangelism from Jonathan Edwards' "Great Awakening" to the revival in Ohio under Finney in pre-Civil War days and the lesser revivals on the frontier in which the moral chaos of the frontier was overcome and a direct religious impulse became the source of every kind of moral discipline. Many of the fruits of the evangelical movement were creative, not only for individuals but for the community. The Great Awakening disturbed the moral complacency of New England

Calvinism, helped Jefferson and Madison to disestablish the church in Virginia, and supplied the fervor for democratic politics from Jefferson to Jackson.

Both the Great Awakening and the later revival under Finney, centering in Oberlin, Ohio, were productive of social as well as of individual creative commitments, saving the individual from undue preoccupation with himself. The Finney revival had a creative offshoot in the anti-slavery impulse. Its abolitionist sentiment was less marred by self-righteous fury than the older abolitionism of Garrison and Phillips.

Nevertheless the evangelical movement did not affect seriously the institution of slavery. It did not prompt evangelical slave-owners to free their slaves, as John Woolman's Quakerism did. It did not even mitigate their prejudices. The Anglican aristocracy of Virginia was less emotional in its pro-slavery thought that the sectarian poor, the Methodists and Baptists, who were probably tempted to their anti-Negro sentiment by their social position between the Negro slaves and the land-owning slave-owners.

The failure of Protestant Evangelicalism to challenge the institution of slavery in those states where it was deeply entrenched may not be due to its specific weakness but to the general failure of any religious impulse to change radically a social climate of any culture. Christian radicalism in the Middle Ages prompted some monasteries to manumit their slaves and it prompted the "lady bountifuls" to be charitable toward the poor. But it did not change feudalism, a product of an infinite variety of social and political forces.

But there were specific weaknesses in Evangelicalism which contributed to its failure on the issue of slavery. Among them were its individualism and its perfectionism. Both of them were the fruits of an undue distinction between "saving grace" and "common grace." For this distinction exalts individual experience above social experience and thus obscures the social factors which redeem the individual from undue self-concern on the one hand, and those factors on the other hand which prevent him from regarding his own life critically. Among the latter, one must mention particularly those social institutions which give one man undue power over his fellowmen, thus aggravating his pride and his sense of power. The social life of man can obviously be both the source of common grace and of demonic evil.

The perfectionism of Evangelicalism has its roots in its individualism and its undue emphasis on the saving grace of religious experience. Thereby all shades of love and self-love which hover between justice and injustice, between tolerable and intolerable forms of social discipline and social corruption are obscured. Either the self is involved in sinful self-regard, or repents and becomes unselfish. The fact that no self is consistently unselfish and that even "redeemed" individuals became vexatious in their pride, if their social situation is such as to encourage the ego, are obvious data of human experience which evangelical perfectionism blandly ignores. Thus every source of social discipline and social corruption is obscured. The soul is dependent upon God alone for "judging" and "forgiving" the self. Naturally man's social nature makes this purely vertical relation impossible. It may help, but not too much, to gather these "saved" individuals into a community of "forgiven sinners" and to insist on higher moral standards in this select community than in the whole society. But the evidence of the relation of Christian congregations to their general communities rather points to the fact that the religious community, whether evangelical or conventional, may have higher standards when there is an uncomplicated relation between the religious impulse and the fidelities of moral life, whether in marriage or in business enterprise. But when the relation is indirect, and social life is subject to a web of pressures and counter-pressures, a discriminate judgment and a critical faculty is more important than the religious impulse to "love God and the neighbor."

If these analyses are at all correct, they point to the fact that the law of love is indeed the basis of all moral life, that it can not be obeyed by a simple act of the will because the power of self-concern is too great, and that the forces which draw the self from its undue self-concern are usually forces of "common grace" in the sense that they represent all forms of social security or responsibility or pressure which prompt the self to bethink itself of its social essence and to realize itself by not trying too desperately for self-realization.

But all these complexities also reveal that the distinction between saving and common grace has been too much emphasized by the religious communities. This emphasis has obscured the true situation of the human self, has made for religious self-righteousness, for a meticulous rather than generous moral ethos, and has prevented any truth about love, grace, and law from being generally understood or practiced.